programed
newswriting

One of the most helpful products of behavioral research in education has been programed instruction.

The method, derived from some of the most dependable findings of learning experiments, has been used in a variety of fields—from first aid, to computer programing, to filling out income tax forms.

Programed instruction can be as useful in journalism/communication as in other fields. The careful, step-by-step approach can lead students on their own to achieve good levels of mastery of difficult topics such as news style.

In a time when many journalism schools are crowded and teachers and students are looking for ways to save precious time for personal interaction, programed instruction may turn out to be a boon, for it promises that students or others, working on their own, can master not only news style, but many other journalistic skills as well.

Wayne A. Danielson

John L. Griffith
University of Florida

Edward G. Weston
University of Florida

programed newswriting

PRENTICE-HALL, INC.
Englewood Cliffs, New Jersey 07632

Library of Congress Cataloging in Publication Data

GRIFFITH, JOHN L (date)
    Programed newswriting.

    (Prentice-Hall basic skills in journalism series)
    1. Journalism—Authorship—Programed instruction.
I. Weston, Edward G., (date) joint author.
II. Title.
PN4775.G74   808′.066′02854   77–12495
ISBN 0–13–730630–X

PRENTICE-HALL BASIC SKILLS IN JOURNALISM SERIES
Wayne A. Danielson, *Editor*

© 1978 *by* PRENTICE-HALL, INC., *Englewood Cliffs, New Jersey 07632*

10   9   8   7   6   5   4   3   2   1

Printed in the United States of America

News clippings in the following frames are printed by permission of
the Associated Press: 1–10 A & B, 1–11 A & B, 1–19, 1–20, 2–8
A & B, 2–11, 3–5, 5–3, 5–9, 5–10, 5–16, 5–17B, 6–5, 6–6,
7–5, 8–1, 8–5, 8–8, 9–9, 9–12, 11–3, 11–9, 11–12, 11–13,
11–14, 12–7, 13–20, 15–8B, 15–15, 15–16, 15–17, 15–22,
15–24 A–C, 15–28, 15–44.

News clippings in the following frames are printed by permission of
United Press International: 3–3, 5–3, 5–9, 5–10, 5–17A, 6–3,
7–18, 9–13, 11–2, 11–5, 11–6, 15–7 A & B, 15–20, 15–35,
15–41.

PRENTICE-HALL INTERNATIONAL, INC., *London*

PRENTICE-HALL OF AUSTRALIA PTY. LIMITED, *Sydney*

PRENTICE-HALL OF CANADA, LTD., *Toronto*

PRENTICE-HALL OF INDIA PRIVATE LIMITED, *New Delhi*

PRENTICE-HALL OF JAPAN, INC., *Tokyo*

PRENTICE-HALL OF SOUTHEAST ASIA PTE. LTD., *Singapore*

WHITEHALL BOOKS LIMITED, *Wellington, New Zealand*

contents

preface

Since the programed approach to learning basic journalistic writing is still unfamiliar to many teachers and students, it may be helpful to indicate what this book is and is not intended to accomplish.

Perhaps most important, this book is not intended to replace the instructor. Neither is it intended to eliminate extensive practice in actual newswriting by the student. We know of no substitute for such practice, particularly when combined with meticulous, thoughtful evaluation of the result by a skilled instructor.

An essential element of instruction is the systematic presentation and illustration of basic conventions of journalistic writing. Yet the more class time devoted to the introduction of basic conventions, the less time there is available for students to practice and instructors to evaluate their efforts. Other areas, such as information gathering, valuable even in an introductory course, may be slighted or omitted because there is simply not enough time.

Thus the purpose of this book is to present basic journalistic writing conventions concisely and in a format that allows the student to work out of class and at his or her pace. The format provides continuous checks on the student's comprehension of the material. The student can begin to apply the basic journalistic conventions immediately, returning as necessary to the book for review.

how to use this book

1. Cover the answer key (the left-hand column) with a bookmark or your hand.
2. Work each frame (each numbered box) before going on to the next.
3. Read carefully. Look up words you don't know.
4. When you complete the frame, uncover the answer key and check your answer.
5. If your answer is right, go on to the next frame.
6. If your answer is wrong, correct it at once. Go back. Reread the frame. Find out what you did wrong. If you can't find your error, make a note of it and ask your teacher for help.
7. When you come to a review test, take it. Then check your answers against the answer key for the test.
8. Learning newswriting is important. Don't try to cover too much material at one time. Pace yourself. Master each section before going on to the next.

acknowledgments

We wish to express our gratitude to United Press International and The Associated Press for permission to reprint the story examples used. Very special thanks go to the 2,000 students in Florida and Illinois who labored with early versions of the book and supplied valuable feedback.

programed
newswriting

Chapter
ONE

news values

1–1   Before sitting down at the typewriter, a newswriter has to decide what's newsworthy in a story situation.

Although there are generally agreed-upon guidelines concerning what's newsworthy, the judgment is a subjective one, and is based on some complex variables.

Before you write your story, you have to determine what's ___newsworthy___ in the story situation.

1–1   newsworthy

1–2   You may have some help. You may receive writing assignments in much the same manner as a professional reporter — a half-sheet of copy paper, with a description of the story and a few brief suggestions on story angles written on it. The teacher may add a few comments, or may sit down with you and discuss the main angles to be covered in the story.

Know what story ___angle___ to cover before you go out to gather information.

1–2   angles

1–3   Newswriting requires some shifting of gears from English composition. There the professor is your sole audience — but in newswriting, your ___aud.___ expands considerably.

1–3   audience

1–4   News *values* determine newsworthiness. Two primary news values are *significance* and *reader interest*.

Persons in the mass media audience read news stories because the stories contain information that is significant and of _____ to them.

1–4   interest

1–5   The extent of reader interest in a news event is affected by

(1)   Location of the event

(2)   Prominence of the persons involved

(3)   Human interest (those elements that have emotional appeal)

(4)   Timeliness (how current the event is)

Significance is determined by the consequences of the news event, its importance, its magnitude and the number of persons affected.

The two major factors in newsworthiness are reader interest and the _____ of the event.

1–5   significance

1–6   Location affects newsworthiness in that a news event close to home is of greater reader interest than a similar event elsewhere.

The news event _____ to home has the greater reader interest.

1–6   close

1–7   Names make news, especially names of well-known persons. For example, a story about the mayor being arrested after a fist fight with

2

the chief of police would draw more reader interest than a story about the regular Saturday night fisticuffs behind the neighborhood bar, because the public officials' _____ would be well known to the readers.

1–7   names

1–8   Human interest covers a broad range of emotional appeals. The following are some human interest elements:

unusualness	suspense
conflict	adventure
humor	sympathy
sex	tragedy
romance	age
progress	animals

1–9   Some stories are based entirely on a human interest element. A story about an 85-year-old man receiving his bachelor's degree is based on the elements of unusualness and age.

Other stories may be based primarily on standard news elements but may still use human interest. Take, for example, the story of a barking dog alerting bystanders that his young master is drowning, leading to a rescue and happy ending. Identify the two primary human interest elements in this example.

A.   _____

B.   _____

1–9   A. age — usually a human interest element only if the story subjects are very young or very old. B. animals — suspense and tragedy are other possibilities.

1–10   What type of human interest is dominant in each of these examples?

A.   _____

B.   _____

A.   LONDON (AP) — Eighty-seven-year-old Percy Dunlop is a teacher in a class by himself — a Mr. Chips who won't say goodbye.

He has started on his 68th year at Star Lane Junior School in the Canning Town area of London. "I don't feel any older than when I first came here in 1905," he said.

He "retired" 22 years ago, but two days after the fond farewells he was back at the request of the local education inspector.

He has taught four generations of some local families.

B.   MIAMI (AP) — An American who lost all he owned in the fall of Saigon and worked as a volunteer aide to help Vietnamese refugees is now living in a flophouse because no one will help him.

"I cannot understand why the American government did not allocate money to help destitute American repatriates," Anthony Conti, 50, said Wednesday.

Conti said he is in a situation similar to that of a refugee but has been unable to find a private or public agency to help him.

1–10   A. unusualness/age

            B. sympathy

1–11   What human interest values are in these stories?

        A. _____

        B. _____

A. MIAMI BEACH (AP) — The unidentified old man who had been held in a mental ward for a week lay listlessly in his bed, then a nurse showed him a newspaper photo of an elderly woman. Tears came to his eyes and he cried "Mamma, mamma."

Minutes later, Rebecca Rosenman, 70, who had sat by her telephone for a week, learned her husband Eddie was well and would soon be returning to her.

EDDIE ROSENMAN'S strange interlude began Dec. 23 when he kissed his wife of 50 years goodbye and left for a 10-minute stroll. He wore the redbanded straw hat that made him a familiar figure among the elderly people who came to live in the sun.

When he did not return, Mrs. Rosenman said, "It was like the ground opened and he fell into it."

Eddie Rosenman has been unable to speak more than a few words since he suffered a stroke sometime ago.

B. MIAMI (AP) — What was to have been a "wedding of the year" in toy poodle circles has been postponed because Champion Taylor's Lulu ran off upon arriving at Miami International Airport.

Lulu, a silver-beige poodle owned by Dorothy Taylor of Huntsville, Ala., was to be matched with Champion Peoples Cafe Brulot. Both are grandpups of the late Champion Silver Sparkle of Sassafras, sire of more than 100 champion show dogs.

Carol Waters of South Miami, owner of the prospective bridegroom, has spent much of her time since Lulu ran away Oct. 24, calling for her on a battery-powered megaphone.

Lulu's value for breeding purposes has been estimated at $4,000 to $10,000. The last time she was seen she was in the middle of the airport field, sitting beside — and ignoring — a jackrabbit.

1–11   A. sympathy/age

    B. unusualness/animals

1–12   You may never hear the term *human interest* in the newsroom. More than likely you'll be assigned to do a *color* story about such events as a political convention or the opening of the public schools in the fall.

Or, your assignment may be a *sidebar,* a story that accompanies the main story of an event. You might cover a hotel fire with a standard news story, and use a sidebar to cover the human interest aspects. For example, interviews with the hotel occupants, especially an old lady sitting on the curb with her canary in its cage beside her, would be good material for a sidebar.

So, rather than being assigned a human interest story, you are likely to be given a color story or a _____.

1–12   sidebar

1–13   Acquainting yourself with human interest elements is important. In many cases you may begin a straight news assignment, then uncover human interest potential in the story.

Even though the story is based on the standard news elements, if there is sufficient human interest, incorporate it in your story. If the human interest angle is strong, it may well deserve more

_____ in the story than the standard news elements.

1–13   emphasis/play

1–14   Newspapers differ in terms of what they consider newsworthy. The newspaper's size is a main factor.

A routine club meeting, an event of minimal news value, might be newsworthy for a weekly or small daily, marginal for a larger daily (a paragraph or two at most would be given if the story is used at all), and not considered by a large daily or a metropolitan newspaper.

Stories of events that are local and timely, such as a 4-H Club meeting or a session of the local stamp club, may be used by weeklies and small dailies. The news values of location and _____ may be sufficient for such stories to be newsworthy to small newspapers.

1–14   timeliness

1–15   Larger dailies and metropolitan newspapers, however, require more than these news values. The addition of any one of the other news values — prominence, human interest, significance — would make the story newsworthy for them.

Timeliness and location, then, do not fully meet the requirements of the larger newspaper. Another news value, such as _____,

or _____ _____ or _____, must be present in the story.

1–15   prominence human
interest significance

1–16   At the 4-H Club meeting, an old friend of the sponsor — the governor of the state — drops in unexpectedly, shakes hands with all the members and talks informally about the importance of farming to the state.

The story of this event has become a much better one because of the added news value of _____.

1–16   prominence

1–17   An expert who is attending the stamp club meeting discovers a rare and valuable stamp in a group purchase the club has just made. The story is now a better one. The writer, rather than composing a routine two or three paragraphs about the meeting, would properly play up the news value of _____.

1–17   unusualness/oddity (human
interest)

1–18   There are many combinations of news values that make a good story. A national figure with something important to say is usually considered newsworthy in any daily newspaper, regardless of size. Assuming timeliness, the other two news values would be

_____ and _____.

5

1–18 prominence significance
(importance, magnitude)

1–19   Human interest may be the sole news value in a story used by dailies of all sizes (again assuming the reporting is timely). Identify the human interest element in the following story:

(AP) — Tiny Fort Morgan, Colo., turned on its Christmas lights for two hours Saturday in tribute to the man who played Santa Claus to thousands of children here for a quarter of a century.

Hubert J. "Red" Rasmussen, who died Christmas Eve of a heart attack at the age of 61, was buried Saturday in Denver.

"For the young people of the community, it is a very definite loss," said Bill Whittier, former manager of the local Chamber of Commerce. "It is also a loss to those older ones of us who still believe in Santa Claus."

Rasmussen, a car salesman who had no children of his own, looked the part he played. He was 6 foot 2 and weighed nearly 275 pounds.

"We're going to miss him an awful lot because he was a symbol of Christmas time for all the kids," Fort Morgan Mayor Glenn B. Morgan said. "He will be missed by the entire community."

The human interest element is _____.

1–19   sympathy

1–20   The main human interest element in the following story is

_____.

FORT LAUDERDALE (AP) — A competency hearing was scheduled Tuesday for two elderly brothers who stashed $90,000 in their filthy, insect-infested home.

Police, acting on a call this week from a worried neighbor, found George Krueger, 89, and his brother Oscar, 82, living alongside ceiling-high piles of garbage and unopened mail.

Police said the brothers, who had a drawer full of $20 bills and bank books, were placed in protective custody and admitted to a psychiatric hospital.

1–20   unusualness

1–21   News values are used by the reporter first to differentiate between what is news and what isn't. Then he uses them to set priorities — to decide how much time to spend on each story. The reporter keeps his editors informed about the big stories. The editors also use news values in determining *story play* — story length, placement and display in the newspaper.

Chapter TWO

the lead

2–1   The beginning of the news story is called the *lead* (pronounced *leed*). This beginning, or _____, must be well written so that it will draw the reader into the story.

2–1	lead

2–2   This book deals mainly with writing straight news stories. The function of the straight news story is to convey information to the reader.

     Another type of story, the feature, may transmit information, but it usually has the additional purpose of entertaining the reader. Writing features is covered in Chapter 15.

     The type of story whose main purpose is to inform the reader is _____ (straight news story/feature story).

2–2	straight news story

2–3   The feature story may convey information and also _____ the reader.

2–3	entertain

2–4   Straight news and features are sometimes called *hard news* and *soft news*. Hard news relates to straight news stories and soft news relates to _____ stories.

2–4	feature

2–5   It is common for straight news leads to give a *summary* of the entire story in the fewest possible words — so it's not surprising that this type of lead is called a _____ lead.

2–5	summary

2–6   Look at this lead:

     Fifteen elderly couples were permitted to return to their homes in the Aldersgate Retirement Center in Orange City to begin the task of cleaning up debris left when waters of a nearby lake flooded their homes Thursday, forcing them to flee.

     It gives a _____ of the entire story.

2–6	summary

2–7   Summary leads are one paragraph long. The lead in frame 2–6 is a single _____ in length and gives a summary of the entire story.

     Is this a summary lead? _____ (yes/no)

2–7	paragraph
	yes

2–8   Which story, A or B, has a summary lead? _____

A. TALLAHASSEE (AP) — Three strong, healthy young men. Each married to an attractive woman. Each the father of a small daughter.

     All dead.

     They were Florida Highway Patrol troopers Claud Baker, 32, Charles Parks, 28, and Ronald Smith, 28.

     Each was murdered in the line of duty this year, gunned down under strikingly similar circumstances.

     COL. LEE SIMMONS, assistant director of the patrol, cannot recall a year when as many troopers were killed on the job.

B. (AP) — Police used tear gas early New Year's Eve to disperse some 2,500 young people who assaulted passersby and smashed windows near the beach strip in Miami Beach.

About 20 miles farther north, Fort Lauderdale police also used tear gas to break up a gathering of young people on the beach.

On Miami Beach, seven people were arrested and five officers slightly injured.

2–8 Story B has a summary lead. The first paragraph summarizes the story.

In A, one paragraph doesn't summarize the story; you don't learn that the men were murdered until paragraph four.

2–9 A summary lead answers the main questions a person might ask when hearing of a particular incident. These questions are called the 5 W's and H: the *who, what, when, where, why* and *how.*

The 5 W's and H represent the main _____ a reader might want answered.

2–9 questions

2–10 Which of the 5 W's and H (who, what, when, where, why and how) are answered in this lead? Label them:

Ⓑ ____ Ⓐ ____ Ⓒ _____
LONDON — The world's major tin producing nations decided after a marathon 15-hour bargaining session Thursday to hold back 10 percent of their exports and stockpile it to maintain the high prices. Ⓓ ____
Ⓔ ____

2–10
A. who
B. what
C. when
D. what
E. why

2–11 Which of the 5 W's and H can you find in this lead?

Ⓐ ____ Ⓑ ____
WASHINGTON (AP) — Because of the fuel pinch, Air National Guard pilots assigned to defend the United States against possible bomber attacks are allowed to fly only when ordered aloft to investigate suspicious planes, a Guard source says. Ⓒ ____ Ⓓ ____
Ⓔ ____

2–11
A. why
B. who
C. when
D. what
E. who

2–12 Many routine stories do not have a strong why and how. Most stories do have the other W's, however, which are the _____, _____, _____ and _____.

2–12 who   what   when   where

2–13 However, in some stories the why or how can be a main element of the lead. This lead emphasizes the how:

In a 4-0 vote Friday, county commissioners reaffirmed their firing of County Health Director Clarence Harrison earlier this month.

This lead emphasizes the _____.

To test the old axiom that says you can always do this job a little bit better than the other guy who has it, Fort Wayne city officials are exchanging jobs every two weeks.

2–13 why

the modified
summary lead

3–1   Most newswriters today are using a lead that is shorter and less formal than the pure summary. We'll call it a *modified summary*.

The modified summary uses only the major W's in the first paragraph. The secondary W's are given in subsequent paragraphs.

The modified summary, then, uses only _____ W's in the first paragraph.

3–1   major/important

3–2   In the modified summary lead not all the 5 W's and H are used in the first paragraph, but no important ones should be _____.

3–2   omitted

3–3   This story illustrates how several topics are handled in summary form:

TALLAHASSEE (UPI) — The Legislature will have a busy session trying to balance a state budget squeezed by the energy crunch, wrestling again with the equal rights amendment for women and fighting a "phantom government" of rule-writing bureaucrats.
That's the view of Senate President Mallory Horne, D-Tallahassee.

3–4   A modified summary of the same story might look like this:

TALLAHASSEE — The Legislature's toughest problem in this session will be trying to balance a state budget squeezed by the energy crunch, says Senate President Mallory Horne, D-Tallahassee.
Other major chores, he said, will be wrestling again with the equal rights amendment for women and fighting a "phantom government" of rule-writing bureaucrats.

Note how in the modified summary a main element is isolated in the lead, and the other elements are brought in immediately in the second paragraph.

3–5   The type of story you are writing will help you determine whether a summary lead or a modified summary lead is more appropriate.

The simple, uncomplicated story often can be handled well with the summary lead. Examples might be a traffic fatality, a supermarket burglary, an obituary or the selection of a speaker for next week's chamber of commerce banquet.

Here are a few more examples. Note the types of story content.

Methods of fighting reading problems of children and adults were introduced to educators from around the state at a Right to Read Conference held in the Kahler Plaza in downtown Lansing.

ANDERSON, Calif. (AP) — Six cars of an Amtrak train loaded with between 300 and 400 holiday passengers derailed near here early today, officials said. Up to 80 passengers were injured, none seriously, they said.

Area businessmen who will advise 34 Junior Achievement companies beginning next week gathered Thursday night for the last of three orientation sessions outlining how some 680 high school students will operate their own businesses.

The summary lead, then, often is appropriate for the _____ type of story.

3–5   simple/uncomplicated

3–6   If your lead becomes too crowded and complicated, however, give the main point in the first paragraph in a concise, readable form and bring in secondary information in the _____ paragraph.

3–6   second/next

3–7   If you have handled only the main point in the first paragraph and have brought in secondary material in the second, the lead would be called a _____   _____ lead.

3–7   modified summary

3–8   Even when your story is a simple one, if the lead is becoming too _____ when written in summary style, use a modified summary lead.

3–8   long/complicated

3–9   In the following example, a great deal of information is jammed into the lead, and comprehension is difficult:

CASA GRANDE, Ariz. — Intense heat and smoke from a mine fire continued to hamper six five-man rescue teams, equipped with oxygen tanks and heat-resistant clothing, in their efforts to rescue David Deeder and an unidentified companion, believed to be trapped 1,200 feet underground by a tunnel cave-in at a trouble-plagued Arizona copper mine.

3–10   In the following version, a modified summary approach is used, and the details of the rescue attempt appear in later paragraphs.

CASA GRANDE, Ariz. — Intense heat and smoke from a mine fire continued to hamper attempts to rescue two men believed to be trapped 1,200 feet underground by a tunnel cave-in in a copper mine.

Six five-man rescue teams, equipped with oxygen tanks and heat-resistant clothing, alternated in attempts to enter the mine, but were driven back by the heat.

A spokesman said the heat was gradually becoming less intense, and crews were expected to reach David Deeder, an assistant mine foreman, and an unidentified second man, as soon as possible.

3–11   Generally, the complicated, multiple-fact story, because of its complexity and length, should be handled with a _____ (summary/modified summary) lead.

3–11   modified summary

3–12   Read this story:

LEESBURG — A 3-year-old boy was listed in fair condition at Leesburg General Hospital Monday after undergoing emergency surgery for an accidental gunshot wound.

According to police, Carlos Williams, son of Mr. and Mrs. Cleveland Williams, 2204 Mispah Ave., was shot at his home about 7:30 a.m. Monday with a .38 caliber revolver, which accidentally discharged when an older brother pulled it from a dresser drawer.

The lead paragraph would become too crowded if it included all three main points: (1) victim's name, (2) when and where, and (3) how he was shot.

Chapter
FOUR

news story
structure

4-1 A common newswriting structure is the *inverted pyramid*. The most important fact, or *climax* of the story, is given at the beginning of the story.

The second most important fact comes second. Remaining facts are placed in the order of diminishing importance.

In the inverted pyramid form, then, the most important fact comes at the _____ (beginning/middle/end).

4-1 beginning

4-2 Study the following diagrams, which show the difference between the inverted pyramid form and the conventional literary (usually chronological) form:

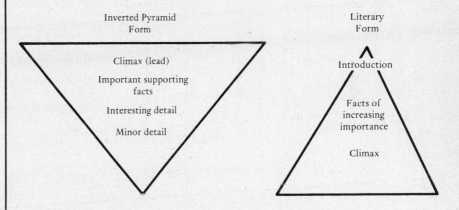

The form used for newswriting is the
_____ _____ form.

4-2 inverted pyramid

4-3 In the inverted pyramid form the main elements of the story (climax) are placed at the beginning; in the literary form these main elements are placed at the _____.

4-3 end

4-4 Notice (from top to bottom in the diagram) the four parts of the inverted pyramid form: lead, important supporting facts, interesting detail and _____ _____.

4-4 minor detail

4-5 In this form the most important information is at the beginning of the story and the _____ important information is at the end.

4-5 least

4-6 Notice that in the inverted pyramid form all the detail and supporting facts in the body of the story give more information about what has been summarized earlier in the _____.

4-6 lead

4-7 Every fact in the lead must be supported later, in detail, in the _____ of the story.

15

4–7   body

4–8   importance/value

4–9   news

4–10   long/crowded

4–11   hard/difficult

4–12   crowded/long

4–13   short

4–14   paragraphs

4–16   one/single

4–17   central   supporting detail

4–8   Information in the inverted pyramid form is ranked in the order of its _____.

4–9   The inverted pyramid form is used in writing most straight _____ stories (hard news), whereas the literary form (the upright pyramid) is often more appropriate for feature stories.

4–10   A summary of information at the beginning of the story is an important component of the inverted pyramid form.

     The newswriter should summarize as much of the story as possible, but he or she should handle it concisely so that sentences and paragraphs don't become too _____.

4–11   When writing a summary lead, the writer has to guard against having a paragraph so long that reading is difficult.

     Short paragraphs are relatively easy to read, whereas long paragraphs are _____ to read.

4–12   Too many ideas and facts in one lead paragraph result in crowding and reduce readability. Writing leads that are too _____ is a poor practice.

4–13   For maximum readability, sentences in the lead should be short. Likewise, paragraphs should be _____.

4–14   Short sentences and short _____ make the lead easier to read.

4–15   Follow this guideline throughout the body of a story: Use short sentences and short paragraphs. Also, choose a simple, easily understood word rather than a long, complicated word.

4–16   Most good leads are one sentence long. Other facts not selected for this single sentence are placed in succeeding paragraphs.

     The writer avoids crowding by using _____-sentence leads.

4–17   To stress the important point and to keep it short, the lead should emphasize the central fact of the story and use only enough supporting detail to make the central fact understandable.

     The _____ fact should be emphasized with enough _____ _____ to make it understandable.

16

review test for chapters 1-4

1. If news values were condensed into two areas, they probably would be reader interest and _____.

2. Names make news, especially the names of _____ persons.

3. A story that accompanies the main story of an event is called a _____.

4. What is the dominant type of human interest in this story?

   _____

   > Brian Inglis, a 30-year-old vegetarian, has painfully learned the truth in the adage that you are what you eat.
   > In his case it's garlic, lots of it, and his eating habits have already cost him his job.

5. There are two human interest elements in the following story. Name them.

   > Orville Schukar, owner of Sug's Super Service Station in Vandalia, Ill., accepts cash, checks and credit cards in payment for services. But Queenie, his top helper, will accept only cash.
   > Queenie is white with a tinge of brown and apparently mostly German shepherd.

   _____ and _____

6. A story that is mainly concerned with entertaining the reader is called a _____ story. News of this type also is called _____ news.

7. The summary lead is _____ paragraph(s) long.

8. The main questions a person might ask about a news event (the famous 5 W's and H) are _____, _____, _____, _____, _____ and _____.

9. Straight news leads give a _____ of the entire story in the fewest possible words.

10. From top to bottom, the four parts of the inverted pyramid form
   are

   A. lead

   B. important _____ facts

   C. interesting detail

   D. _____ detail

11. Which of the following is more readable? _____

   A. The federal government has been ordered for the first
   time to pay damages growing out of illegal surveillance.

   B. Dr. Arthur Squires, professor of chemical
   engineering at City College of New York, said
   Wednesday his team of experts would demonstrate a new
   coal gasification process to representatives of American
   industry next week at a New York conference.

12. A crowded, complicated lead can be avoided by using the
   _____   _____ lead.

13. Most good leads are _____ sentence long, with emphasis on
   the _____ fact.

answers

1. significance
2. well-known/prominent
3. sidebar
4. unusualness
5. unusualness; animals
6. feature; soft
7. one
8. who, what, when, where, why, how
9. summary
10. B. important supporting facts
    D. minor detail
11. Example A is more readable because it is more concise.
12. modified summary
13. one; central

Chapter FIVE

of the lead

5–1 In the inverted pyramid form, the 5 W's in the lead are given in the order of their importance. Therefore, the W considered most _____ is placed early in the lead.

5–1 important

5–2 This element is the lead feature, and in this book it will be called the *feature of the lead.*

The best item of your story, which will be called the _____ of the _____, should be placed early in the lead.

5–2 feature of the lead

5–3 In each of the following examples, the feature of the lead is italicized. Note that each italicized section is a capsule version of the story.

TALLAHASSEE (AP) — *Vandals have cut down state-planted roadside trees* — some in front of billboard signs — and damaged many more, State Transportation Secretary Ed Mueller said Tuesday.

Some incidents of tree cutting, and a few instances of spraying roadside growth with herbicides, have occurred . . . .

ANTALYA, Turkey (UPI) — *A powerful earthquake shook Southwest Turkey* Wednesday, leveling entire villages and killing scores of persons, including women and children trapped in their homes.

Officials in Burdur, near the center of the quake, said at least 65 persons died in Burdur and two nearby villages. They said the death toll in Burdur was 25 and at least 40 died in the villages of . . . .

5–4 This concept of the feature of the lead is extremely important.
Learn to identify the most important element of the story, so that you place it correctly in the lead.

Review the examples in frame 5–3. In both stories the feature of the lead comes at the _____ (beginning/middle/end) of the first sentence.

5–4 beginning

5–5 This most important W, or feature of the lead, may be placed at the beginning of the first sentence in some stories. However, the feature of the lead should not be at the very beginning if it creates awkward and illogical sentence order.
Read the following lead:

The FBI disclosed Monday its annual budget runs to half a billion dollars, including $80 million for secret counterspy and crime-busting operations.

The feature of the lead is not at the very beginning to avoid awkward and illogical _____ _____.

5–5 sentence order

5–6 The feature of the lead is properly placed in the first sentence in a manner that achieves natural and logical sentence order.

It must be in the _____ sentence of the story, or the result is a *buried lead,* a major newswriting error.

5–6   first

5–7   importance/value

5–8   what   who

5–11   when   where

5–13   who   what

5–7   After the feature of the lead is placed in the first sentence, the remaining W's should be given in the order of their _____.

5–8   Since most news stories deal with things or persons, the W's most used for features of the lead are _____ and _____.

5–9   Look at these examples of *who* leads:

VIENNA, Austria (AP) — Two Arab terrorists, calling themselves the Eagles of the Palestinian Revolution, raided a train coach carrying 37 Russian Jews and seized four hostages Friday.

TALLAHASSEE (UPI) — State Rep. Van B. Poole, R-Fort Lauderdale, introduced a bill yesterday to forbid hitchhiking — and the picking up of hitchhikers.
Poole billed his proposal as a "rape, murder and robbery-prevention bill."

5–10   Here are some examples of *what* leads:

CATANIA, Sicily (UPI) — Two streams of lava advanced toward the town of Fornazzo on the side of Mount Etna Tuesday, searing acres of fertile farmland and destroying a half-dozen cottages.

WASHINGTON (AP) — Successful Soviet tests of multiple nuclear warheads that can be aimed at separate targets could give the Soviet Union a clear missile striking edge over the United States by the 1980s, says . . . .

5–11   The who or the what is generally the most important W, and is used most often for the feature of the lead. The least important W's are the when and the where.

Then, the W's seldom used as the feature of the lead because of their unimportance are the _____ and the _____.

5–12   If the when or where were used as the feature of the lead, the writing would be amateurish, because the emphasis would be on the unimportant W's.
Don't begin your story with
In Civic Auditorium next Friday the Blank Association will . . . .
or
On Monday, Aug. 16, the Blank Association will . . . .

5–13   Rather than emphasizing the when and where for features of the lead, use these W's: _____ and _____.

5–14   Lead sentences may begin with the information source if that person's name is meaningful to the readers — that is, if the person has some degree of prominence. Read this example:

Mayor Thomas Ruff said Tuesday he doesn't believe the controversy over his income tax status will harm his political career because "the overwhelming majority of people understand there was nothing wrong."

22

The source is at the beginning and for readers in that city the source is a

_____ person.

5–14   prominent/well-known

5–15   Some leads may begin with an organization as the source, as in this example:

The Air Force announced Wednesday its trouble-plagued F-4 fighter-bomber has resumed flying after being grounded temporarily since a May 2 crash.

This practice lends authority to the statement being made and orients the reader somewhat. When deciding whether to use this style, remember that the key information should not be unduly delayed.

The source, or authority, at the beginning of this lead

_____ the reader as to what the story is about.

5–15   orients/informs

5–16   Here are some other examples in which the organization is given at the beginning of the lead.

A committee studying problems of the aged Tuesday recommended the federal government provide a minimum annual income for every elderly person in the United States.
The recommendation was one of many made by 14 committees during the Florida State White House Conference on Aging at Orlando's Park Plaza Hotel.

PHILADELPHIA (AP) — The Associated Press Managing Editors Association has told a Senate Judiciary subcommittee that if attacks on America's free press are successful "deep trouble for the nation lies ahead."
In a statement distributed at the APME's 38th annual meeting, which concludes Friday, the editors said they hope to find allies in Congress to help the news media . . . .

Note how this orients the reader as to what the content of the story will be.

5–17   Underline the feature of the lead in each of the following:

A. SILVER SPRING, Md. (UPI) — An undercover policeman was fatally shot and a second agent was wounded Saturday night when two suspected drug dealers opened fire on the officers during a "drug buy" in a hotel room.

B. A semi-trailer truck leaking propane gas exploded shortly before dawn today, destroying several buildings and sending flames shooting 75 feet in the air.

5–17   A. An undercover policeman was fatally shot and a second agent was wounded
B. A semi-trailer truck leaking propane gas exploded

5–18   Look again at the examples in frame 5–17. Count the first 15 words in each. In most stories, if the feature of the lead is handled correctly you should have a good idea of the gist of the story, the outcome, in the first 15 words or so.

Do these leads pass the 15-word test? _____ (yes/no)

5–18   yes

Chapter SIX

advance and follow-up stories

6-1 Now for advance and follow-up stories. If your lead concerns a meeting or event in the future (advance), don't emphasize that a meeting *will be held*. Instead, the feature of the lead should include *specific things* that will take place.

So, in your story of a future event, the feature of the lead should be

_____ .

6-1 what will take place (specific things)

6-2 Read these versions of an advance story:

A. The beautification committee of the Springfield Central Business District Inc. will meet today to organize a campaign to collect funds for the Orange Avenue tree planting project.

B. A campaign to collect funds for the Orange Avenue tree planting project of the Springfield Central Business District Inc. will be organized at a meeting of the group's beautification committee today.

C. A meeting of the beautification committee of the Springfield Central Business District Inc. will be held today. The group will organize a campaign to collect funds for the Orange Avenue tree planting project.

Which best handles the future event for an advance story? _____

6-2 Example B is good; the feature deals with specific things that will take place.
Example A is also satisfactory; although emphasis is on the committee at the beginning, the last part of the sentence ties in the events that will take place. The sentence is direct and elements are in logical order.
Example C is the weakest story. Note that it's a ''will be held'' type with the key information unnecessarily delayed to a second sentence.

6-3 Follow the principle of using specifics for the feature of the lead when reporting past events.
When writing about past meetings or events, tell the *outcome;* don't emphasize the event itself. Examine this story:

TALLAHASSEE (UPI) — Ecologists warned of "irreparable damage" to nature Monday while local government officials spoke in favor of plans to drill for oil in the Big Cypress Swamp.
Both groups appeared before Cabinet aides gathering information so they can recommend to their bosses a policy for the state on drilling oil in the wilderness.

The two features captured in the lead sentence are

A. _____

B. _____

6-3 A. ecologists warning of damage
B. local officials favoring drilling
Notice that no emphasis is given to the conference ''being held.'' The fact that it was a conference is delayed to the third paragraph.

6-4 Which best handles the past event? _____

A. LEXINGTON — The Senate Health, Welfare and Institutions Committee Tuesday presented a report about sanitary conditions in state restaurants. It said conditions are so poor in at least 34 counties — including some of the most populous — that they pose a serious health menace.

B. LEXINGTON — The Senate Health, Welfare and Institutions Committee met Tuesday. Main business was a report that sanitary conditions in restaurants in at least 34 Kentucky counties are very poor. The situation poses a serious health menace, the committee indicated.

C. LEXINGTON — Sanitary conditions are so poor in restaurants in at least 34 Kentucky counties — including some of the most populous — that they pose a serious health menace, a Senate committee reported Tuesday.
The report by the Health, Welfare and Institutions Committee said . . . .

D. LEXINGTON — The Senate Health, Welfare and Institutions Committee said Tuesday that sanitary conditions are so poor in restaurants in at least 34 counties — including some of the most populous — that they pose a serious health menace.

6–4   **C.** Congratulations! Take the rest of the week off. The lead has key information in the first part of the lead sentence.

D. Some writers would handle it this way, using the concept we've discussed of beginning with the organization to orient readers.

A. No. First sentence doesn't give enough of *outcome*.

6–5   Look at the lead of the following story. It features the *outcome*, the *result*. It doesn't lead off with the fact that mental health workers *met today*.

CHICAGO (AP) — Illinois mental health workers called off a strike scheduled today pending completion of a wage study ordered by Gov. Richard B. Ogilvie.

6–6   Now look at this lead:

LOS ANGELES (AP) — The president of the Air Line Pilots Association urged the news media Saturday to voluntarily play down stories on successful skyjackings and play up unsuccessful ones.
"I think if the press were to play down skyjackings which are successful and only play up those which are unsuccessful, eventually the depraved mind that undertakes these things would get the idea that no one ever gets away with it," Donald McBain said.

This lead also plays up the *result*. It doesn't feature the fact that the captain testified before the subcommittee, or that the subcommittee met.

In writing of past events, you should emphasize the _____ of that event.

6–6   outcome/result

Chapter
SEVEN

the speech story

7-1 what was said

7-1 The principle of emphasizing results or outcomes is used in writing speech stories. In covering a speech, the writer does not emphasize that a speech was given (the "will be held" problem). Rather, he or she emphasizes _____.

7-2 In writing the lead for a speech story, the reporter can summarize the speaker's opinion on the topic or can lead with the important point or points made by the speaker. This can be done with a paraphrase, direct quote or a combination of the two (a partial quote).

The speech story lead can emphasize the important point or points made in the speech, or it can summarize the speaker's _____ on the topic.

7-2 opinion

7-3 Read this lead:

Adequate health care is not being delivered to the elderly, the chairman of a Florida task force told a U.S. Senate hearing Monday in Orlando.

It summarizes an opinion of the speaker and is done in _____ (paraphrase/direct quote/partial quote) form.

7-3 paraphrase

7-4 The lead must capture the important and newsworthy elements of the speech, usually the speaker's opinion or an important point.

The effective speech story lead, then, emphasizes the _____ elements of the speech.

7-4 important/newsworthy

7-5 Read these speech stories:

WASHINGTON — The public drinking water supplies of this nation are a success story growing stagnant, a former federal official said Tuesday.

Because of a federal-state program begun 60 years ago, said Charles C. Johnson Jr., "epidemics traceable to water-borne diseases are no longer a part of our way of life."

But now, he said, efforts to maintain safe water supplies have started to sag.

CYPRESS GARDENS (AP) — "It is going a little too far to say that a reporter must be allowed to hear any discussion between two officials," said Gov. Reubin Askew, giving his thoughts on the controversial Sunshine Law.

Although he supports the Government-in-the-Sunshine Law, Askew said he "respectfully disagrees with some of the interpretations" that have been placed on it.

ASKEW spoke to about 150 persons at the Florida Press Association spring convention banquet Friday night.

Both stories capture the speaker's _____ on the subject.

7-5 opinion

7-6 The direct quotation should be used sparingly in speech story leads. A paraphrase often more effectively captures the speaker's opinion or important points. However, use the direct quotation if it is as effective as a _____.

7–6   paraphrase

7–7   When writing direct quote leads, be careful not to distort by overemphasis or change the speaker's meaning by removing a quote from context.

Overemphasis or removing a quote from context can _____ the original meaning.

7–7   change/distort

7–8   If the speaker is prominent — the name is meaningful to readers — use the same technique as in the story in which the source is prominent. You can _____ the story with the name.

7–8   begin/start

7–9   In this example, the name is given first and is followed immediately by the key statement:

Mayor Leonard Day saluted local law enforcement officials Tuesday, and said their daily efforts are nearly "superhuman."

This lead starts with a name because the source of the statement is so _____.

7–9   prominent/well-known

7–10   For the speech lead it's also possible to combine the two forms, the paraphrase and the direct quotation. This is called a *partial quote*. The partial quote requires careful organization if it is to be easy to read and understand.

A combination of direct quote and paraphrase is called a _____ _____.

7–10   partial quote

7–11   Organization is the key to the effective use of the partial quote. To make the partial quote easy to read and understand, the writer must _____ it carefully.

7–11   organize

7–12   It is common to use the second paragraph to wrap up secondary W's, such as what the occasion was, to whom the speech was given, and possibly a general when and where.

_____ that are not important enough to include in the lead paragraph may be handled in the second paragraph.

7–12   W's/facts

7–13   After the second paragraph has been written, the rest of the speech story should concentrate on the speech itself. Typically a combination of direct quotation paragraphs and paraphrased paragraphs is used. Some partial quotes can be used and usually are effective in providing variety.

_____ _____ can be used in the body of the story to break the monotony of paragraphs of direct quotation and paraphrase.

7–13   partial quotes

7–14   Most speech stories use about twice as much paraphrased material as direct quote material.

You properly would have more of the _____ (quoted/paraphrased) material in your story.

7–14   paraphrased

7–15   As with most news stories, the follow-up speech story should be written in the _____ _____ form, with the climax at the beginning and the least important information at the end.

7–15   inverted pyramid

7–16   Study this example:

After being chosen Teacher of the Year for the second straight year, the youngest professor on the Lee College faculty said his selection proves "students are tired of being taught by gray-haired geriatrics."

Dr. Ralph Anderson, 26, received no applause following his acceptance speech Tuesday to nearly 100 college faculty and administrators.

The lead is a _____ (paraphrase/direct quote/partial quote).

7–16   partial quote

7–17   In the story in frame 7–16, what facts are delayed until the second paragraph?

A. _____

B. _____

7–17   A.   source's name
B.   what the occasion was

7–18   The speech story form can be used for similar stories — the interview, the press conference and the panel discussion. Examine this story:

MONTEGO BAY, Jamaica (UPI) — Arizona's Sen. Barry Goldwater said this weekend the American people should be told the United States is inferior to the Soviet Union in all military areas except experience.

In an interview at the Trvall Hotel where he is vacationing, Goldwater said the United States' being behind the Soviet Union in military power had been known for at least 18 months, but the American people have not been told.

You are told in the second paragraph that this is a/an _____ story.

7–18   an interview

7–19   Always tell the reader the circumstances under which the information is obtained.

As is true in many speech, press conference or interview stories, the occasion (circumstances) is given in the _____ paragraph in the story in frame 7–18.

7–19   second

7–20   Material on organizing information in the body of the story is given in the section on quotes and attribution in Chapter 13. If you will be writing speech stories soon, look at that material now.

Chapter
EIGHT

the blind lead

Chapter
NINE

newswriting conventions

9-1 Names of persons involved in the news incident should be included in your story. Be sure the names are spelled correctly.

On first reference, both first and last names should be used. If the person is not prominent, the middle initial should also be used.

So, in a lead that begins, "Mayor Cooper announced today . . . ," the name is used _____ (correctly/incorrectly).

9-1   incorrectly

9-2 Newspapers differ on the style used for names — especially women's names — after first reference. For names of men, wire service style (and the style of most newspapers) calls for last name only after first reference; women's names should be preceded by *Miss* or *Mrs.* Some papers use *Ms.* for both married and unmarried women, especially if requested to do so. A few papers use last names only after first reference for both men and women.

Since style on this question varies from paper to paper and is changing rapidly, be prepared to adjust to the style preferences of your teacher or editor. On this and other style questions, all writers and editors on a paper must follow the same conventions to avoid inconsistency.

9-3 Most papers use only the last names of men after first reference. Common exceptions are the use of *Mr.* with *Mr. and Mrs.* combinations, and with *the Rev. Mr.* Some papers use *Mr.* with the name of the incumbent president of the United States and in obituaries

Most men, however, are referred to after first reference only by their _____ names.

9-3   last

9-4 Which of the following *first* references are *incorrect?* _____
_____

    A. John A. Jones
    B. Mr. Anderson
    C. Mrs. McDonald
    D. Smith

9-4   B, C, D

9-5 According to wire service style, which of the following *second* references are *incorrect?* _____

    A. Mr. Williams
    B. Williams
    C. Mrs. Beemer
    D. Beemer

9-5   A, D

9-6 Identify all persons mentioned in your story. Never drop a name into your story without some kind of _____.

10-1   There is little difference between newswriting and good writing in general. Newswriting places special emphasis on directness, conciseness, simplicity and clarity.

In newswriting, write the way people *talk* rather than the way they write. Since people don't _____ in complicated sentences, don't use such sentences in your news stories.

10-1   talk/speak

10-2   The most natural order for conversationally styled news sentences is this: subject, verb, object.

>   Illinois mental health workers called off a strike scheduled today.

>   Mueller said today's taxes are hardly a burden.

Include such constructions as participial or prepositional phrases occasionally for variety. However, use them sparingly in leads.

Most sentences in news stories should be in

_____, _____, _____ order.

10-2   subject   verb   object

10-3   Which of these examples shows the best sentence order for a news lead?

A.   After hearing skeptical challenges by nutrition experts, participants in a two-day Stanford University symposium remained undecided Tuesday concerning the use of vitamin C in combatting the common cold.

B.   Advocates and opponents of the use of vitamin C in battling the common cold appear unable to decide on the substance's effectiveness.

10-3   Example B is better. The A lead begins with a phrase.

10-4   You've learned that brevity and directness are important in leads. The principles are equally important in the sentences you use throughout the story.

Concise sentences are _____ to read and understand than ones with unnecessary words.

10-4   easier

10-5   The newswriter eliminates deadwood — words and phrases that take up valuable space but add nothing.

One way to eliminate deadwood is to omit articles *(the, an, a)* if the sentence reads correctly without them. Articles can be omitted in the following examples:

>   ~~The~~ tickets will go on sale Monday.

>   Baker said training ~~the~~ representatives this term would orient them to ~~the~~ available university services.

>   ~~The~~ funding of this program has not been approved.

10-6   Some articles, however, cannot be omitted. The sentence, ''Team cut through 35 feet of ice on glacier'' needs to be written as ''The team cut through 35 feet of ice on the glacier.''

Articles frequently can be omitted before plural nouns:

Doctors say his chances are slim.

Prison officials would not talk with reporters.

10-7 Delete unnecessary articles in the following sentences:

A. The independent dealers may raise their prices beginning Monday.

B. The experts and volunteer workers uncovered remnants of barracks used by the Roman soldiers once based in Chester.

C. The difference between a tankful of 87 octane and 95 octane gas can reach $1.

10-7 A. ~~The~~ independent dealers
B. ~~The~~ experts by ~~the~~ Roman soldiers
C. Sentence is correct.

10-8 Another form of wordiness is redundancy, or needless repetition. In conversation you might hear something called *a true fact*. Since all facts are true by definition, the statement is redundant.

Don't say the same thing twice. Which of the following are redundancies? _____

A. The house was newly painted.

B. It was a proved fact.

C. She gave birth to two twins.

10-8 B, C

10-9 Let's try a few more. Which are redundant? _____

A. The factory was completely destroyed.

B. It was a very unique concept.

C. She gave birth to a baby girl.

D. It was a strange encounter.

10-9 There are redundancies in A (destruction is complete), in B (*unique* means the only one of its kind; the word cannot be modified), and in C (all persons are babies at birth).

10-10 Some redundancies are more difficult to spot. Underline the redundant words.

A. The meeting will begin at 8 p.m. tonight.

B. He is currently chairman of the membership committee.

10-10 A. The abbreviation *p.m.* means "at night."
B. *Currently* is usually redundant if the sentence is in the present tense.

10-11 Here are a few examples of other types of wordiness:

A. The conference will be ~~held~~ Monday.

B. He received ~~the sum of~~ $50.

C. It was damaged in the flood ~~which occurred~~ in 1973.

47

D. The committee met for a brief period of time. (Or, *The committee met briefly.*)

E. The new traffic light will be located at the corner of Washington and Elm.

F. They discussed whether or not to nominate him.

G. The committee reported it had not yet completed the plan.

10–12   Edit or revise to eliminate the unnecessary constructions:

A. The debate finally ended late this morning.

B. Little construction was reported during the winter months.

C. Dr. Dale Reid will speak on the subject of ecology.

D. Plans for the structure have already begun.

E. The carton fell off of the loading dock.

F. A priest gave last rites to the victim pinned in one of the crushed cars.

G. The grain elevator burned down.

10–12   A. ~~finally~~
B. ~~months~~
C. ~~the subject of~~ (Or, *Dr. Dale Reid will speak about ecology.*)
D. ~~already~~
E. ~~of~~
F. Sentence is correct.
G. ~~down~~

10–13   Edit or revise:

A. Students will be going to the conference Friday.

B. The miners' leaders will meet on Thursday to discuss their next move.

C. Bohlen began his 40-year diplomatic career in 1929.

D. City Manager R. E. Johnson submitted his resignation today.

E. Lasky served as county chairman in 1972.

10–13   A. will go
B. ~~on~~
C. Sentence is correct.
D. resigned today
E. was county chairman

10–14   Names of states following cities are omitted if the city is well known and will not be confused with another city of the same name. Edit the following sentences:

A. The next conference will be in Chicago, Ill., Sept. 13–15.

B. Wiseman was born in Salt Lake City, Utah.

C. He plans to begin a law practice in Paris, Texas.

10–14   A. Delete *Ill*.
           B. Delete *Utah*.
           C. Sentence is correct.

10–15   Use simple, precise words rather than large words that not all your readers can understand. Even if a large word can be understood readily, the shorter word is preferred. For example, *drink* is preferred to *beverage*.

Pick the best word in each pair:

died/passed away

flood/inundate

interred/buried

improved/ameliorated

10–15 died
         flood
       buried
    improved

10–16   Many newswriting books include long lists of commonly misused words and expressions. Here we'll discuss some of the worst offenders that appear consistently in student writing.

Alot, a word that appears often in direct quotes, is actually two words, *a lot*. But _____ (a lot/alot) of errors are made in its use.

10–16 a lot

10–17   *Anxious* comes from the word *anxiety* and implies worry. It is not a synonym for *eager,* which implies anticipation.

A youngster would probably be _____ (anxious/eager) for Christmas to come.

10–17 eager

10–18   *Capital* refers to the city; *capitol* refers to the building.

Springfield is the _____ (capital/capitol) of Illinois.

10–18 capital

10–19   Delete the final *s* from *towards* and *afterwards*.

The man walked _____ (toward/towards) the building.

10–19 toward

10–20   *Media* is the plural of *medium*.

Smith described television as a _____ (media/medium) of images rather than of information.

10–20 medium

10–21   *Farther,* not *further,* refers to distance.

It is 50 miles _____ (farther/further) to the city.

10–21 farther

10–22   Select the preferred term in the following:

A. He was _____ (anxious/eager) to begin.

B. She said she learned _____ (a lot/alot) from the meeting.

C. He described it _____ (afterward/afterwards) as a horrible experience.

D. They're planning a tour of the _____ (capital/capitol) building.

E. The broadcast media _____ (is/are) increasingly important in politics.

F. The committee will look into the matter _____ (farther/further).

10–22 A. eager
           B. a lot
           C. afterward
           D. capitol
           E. are
           F. further

10–23 *It's* is a contraction meaning "it is." With the apostrophe, it means *it is*.

Its is a pronoun showing possession: "The committee submitted *its* final report."

One leading department store doubled _____ (it's/its) detective force to guard against shoplifters.

10–23 its

10–24 *People* refers only to large populations of a city, state or nation. *Persons* is the correct word for smaller groups.

Eight _____ (persons/people) were injured in the accident.

10–24 persons

10–25 *Over* is not a synonym for *more than*. *Over* means "above"; *more than* means "in excess of."

_____ (More than/Over) $100,000 has been pledged for the United Way drive.

10–25 More than

10–26 Children are *reared,* not *raised.*

Jones was _____ (raised/reared) in Illinois.

10–26 reared

10–27 *Collide* refers to moving objects; use *hit* or *struck* when only one object is moving.

The car _____ (struck/collided with) the building.

10–27 struck

10–28 Review, then complete these sentences:

A. Johnson was _____ (reared/raised) in Indiana.

B. _____ (Over/More than) 50 _____ (persons/people) joined the protest.

C. The bus pulled out and _____ (struck/ collided with) a passing car.

D. The county attorney assured the commission it could withdraw _____ (it's/its) application.

E. Rockledge said _____ (it's/its) apparent that property owners are concerned.

10–28   A. reared
B. More than _____ persons
C. collided with
D. its (pronoun)
E. it's (contraction)

10–29   The next few frames deal with elements that often are troublesome to the beginning newswriter. First, we'll look at the "there will be" problem.

If you are tempted to begin a sentence with "There will be" — don't. It clutters the prime space of your sentence (the beginning) with waste words. Rewrite "There will be" beginnings, especially in leads.

When your sentence begins with "There will be" you should _____ it.

10–29   rewrite

10–30   The "There will be" construction is easy to revise. Look at the following lead:

There will be a competency hearing here Tuesday for two elderly brothers who hid $90,000 in their filthy, insect-infested home.

Here's a revision:

A competency hearing is scheduled Tuesday for two elderly brothers who hid $90,000 in their filthy, insect-infested home.

Rewrite the following lead:

There will be a meeting Monday of more than 70 Florida business leaders to begin a 12-week study of state government operations in an attempt to find out how costs can be cut.

Write your version here:

10–30   More than 70 Florida business leaders Monday will begin a 12-week study of state government operations in an attempt to find out how costs can be cut.

10–31   Another problem is the adjective phrase "__-year-old" preceding a noun, as in "the 14-year-old boy." Notice that the phrase is properly punctuated with two hyphens.

Punctuation remains the same if the phrase follows the name and still modifies a noun: "Johnnie, the 14-year-old son of Mr. and Mrs. J. E. Smith."

However, if *year old* is changed to *years old* following a name, it is not hyphenated: "Johnnie, 14 years old." With this construction the preferred style is to use only the numerical age: "Johnnie, 14."

Edit any incorrect usage:

A. Smith, 81-years-old.

B. an 81 year old man

C. Smith, an 81-year-old medical doctor

10–31 A. 81 years old

B. 81-year-old

10–32 As a matter of style, the semicolon is rarely used in newswriting. The writer would probably revise this sentence:

About $200,000 is being sought to finance the study; some matching funds could decrease that amount.

A dash can be substituted for the semicolon, but the dash should be used sparingly:

About $200,000 is being sought to finance the study — some matching funds could decrease that amount.

Or, the sentence could be broken into two sentences:

About $200,000 is being sought to finance the study. Some matching funds could decrease that amount.

Too many short sentences in a story result in choppy writing. Therefore, if the two sentences are short and the content is closely related, a comma and a conjunction may be used to replace the semicolon:

About $200,000 is being sought to finance the study, but some matching funds could decrease that amount.

10–33 Revise the following sentence to eliminate the semicolon:

Using a gasoline with too low an octane can damage a car's engine; using a gasoline with too high an octane is a waste of money.

10–33 Possible solutions:
engine. Using . . . .
engine, but . . . .
engine — using . . . .

10–34 The main use of the semicolon is to separate a name and its accompanying information from other names in a series.

A. Harold Erickson, 31, of 522 N. Mason Blvd.;
Mary Evans, 35, of 18 W. Elm Ave.; . . . .

B. John Farmer, Oklahoma City; Martin Gallat,
Tulsa; . . . .

In example A, the unit made up of the name, age and

_____ of each person is separated from the others in the series by a semicolon.

In example B, the name and _____ are followed by a semicolon.

10–34 address
city/home town

10–35 There are many kinds of series:

Other states above the national unemployment average were California, 7.3 percent; Connecticut, 6.1; Florida, 6.2; . . . .

Panel members include Dr. Jaime L. Eria, professor of pediatrics; Dr. Melvin Greer, chairman of the department of neurology; . . . .

A series is common in obituaries:

Mrs. Lindsey is survived by two sons, Richard, San Antonio, and John, Dallas; a daughter, Mrs. Carolyn Quinn, San Francisco; a sister, Mrs. Marilyn Tifton, El Paso; and several grandchildren.

52

The semicolon is used to separate a _____ and its accompanying _____ from the other elements in a series.

10–35	name	information

10–36   There is nothing mysterious about the rules for using commas. Perhaps the most common error is the omission of the comma after an identification:

> WRONG: Maj. Gen. Ernest H. Smith, a St. Louis resident watched the National Guard's annual review.
> RIGHT: Maj. Gen. Ernest H. Smith, a St. Louis resident, watched the National Guard's annual review.

When a name is followed by an identification or any parenthetical element, that identification or element is set off with commas before and _____.

10–36	after

10–37   Remember this rule: Commas come in pairs when used with identifications. Read this name and identification:

Trudy Pratt a volunteer with the local humane society received an anonymous phone call about the dead cows.

The first comma should come after *Pratt,* and the second comma of the pair should come after the word _____.

When used with identifications, commas come in _____.

10–37	society
	pairs

10–38   Commas also are used to set off the name of a state following a city:

He was born 64 years ago in Osyka, Miss., and moved to Atlanta in 1921.

Since commas set off the state, before and after, we are still following the rule of commas coming in _____.

10–38	pairs

10–39   Commas are not used when a formal title precedes a name:

Chief Deputy W. H. Phillips said the inmates escaped during the night.
To write "Sheriff, Joseph Rogers, said the search . . ." is incorrect.

So, even if the title is more than one word, no commas are used if the title _____ the name.

10–39	precedes

10–40   The comma is used in figures of one thousand and more: 1,000; $12,000.

The comma in a _____ makes it easier to read.

10–40	figure/numeral

10–41   When a numeral begins a sentence, it must be spelled:

Fifteen minutes after the explosion a man called the police.

The numeral must be _____ when it begins a sentence.

10–41	spelled

review test for chapter 10

1.   The preferred order for news sentences is _____.

2.   In which lead is the sentence order better? _____.

        A. An alternative for a massive annexation proposal hotly opposed Monday in the first public hearing is being compiled by City Manager David Walker.

        B. Hotly opposed Monday in the first public hearing, an alternative for a massive annexation proposal is being compiled by City Manager David Walker.

3.   Names of states following well-known cities are _____ (included/omitted).

4.   The general rule is to omit articles before _____

5.   Which lead is better? _____

        A. A demonstration of Emergency Medical Service telemetry equipment is scheduled . . .

        B. There will be a demonstration of Emergency Medical Service telemetry equipment . . .

6.   Which paragraph best illustrates proper news style? _____

        A. Boyd said his "first conscious memory" of the memorandum was finding it lying on his desk at the court in mid-July of 1973; he said he did not recall if it was in a file or beside a file.

        B. Boyd said his "first conscious memory" of the memorandum was finding it lying on his desk at the court in mid-July of 1973. He said he did not recall if it was in a file or beside a file.

7.   Punctuate correctly:

      New officers are Betty Allen Chicago president James Woodruff Indianapolis vice president Janice Smith Milwaukee treasurer.

8.   Correct any comma errors in the following:

        A. The boat found in the Gulf Stream originally belonged to James Oletto, a Chicago developer agents said.

B. Henry Tonkin, district forecaster with the National Weather Service said the county has had 3.34 inches of rain so far this year.

C. City Manager Harold Stabler defended the increase in water rates.

D. Ceremonies at Camp Blanding, Fla. began with a 12-gun salute, included a parade of 2000 National Guardsmen and concluded with a helicopter flyover.

answers

1. subject, verb, object
2. A (B begins with a phrase.)
3. omitted
4. plural nouns
5. A
6. B
7. New officers are Betty Allen, Chicago, president; James Woodruff, Indianapolis, vice president; Janice Smith, Milwaukee, treasurer.
8. **A.** The boat found in the Gulf Stream originally belonged to James Oletto, a Chicago developer, agents said.

   B. Henry Tonkin, district forecaster with the National Weather Service, said the county has had 3.34 inches of rain so far this year.

   C. Sentence is correct.

   D. Ceremonies at Camp Blanding, Fla., began with a 12-gun salute, included a parade of 2,000 National Guardsmen and concluded with a helicopter flyover.

Chapter ELEVEN

bridge paragraphs

11–1 You might think of the second paragraph of a story as a *bridge* between the essential information in the first paragraph and the details later in the story. Thus the second paragraph is sometimes called the _____.

11–1 bridge

11–2 In the example that follows, the italicized material in the bridge gives the reader secondary W's not used in the lead. In this case, the where and the why elements are valuable for an understanding of the story, but they are not essential for the lead.

BEIRUT (UPI) — Premier Rashid Solh has resigned after six months in office, angrily accusing the rightwing Phalangist party of plunging Lebanon into a new round of political instability.

Solh, *the latest victim of Lebanon's precarious political system, announced his resignation yesterday in an emotional speech before parliament.*

Solh accused Phalangist militiamen of starting last month's bloody clashes with Palestinian guerrillas. Hundreds of persons were killed or wounded in the fighting.

11–3 In which paragraph do the secondary W's, the when and the where, appear? _____

CHICAGO (AP) — It isn't the violence on television which creates violent children but the way their parents bring them up, two child development experts say.

However, they are critical of the passivity of children who spend hour after hour watching television.

The two experts made their comments during a workshop at the annual meeting of the American Association of Psychiatric Services for Children, Inc., held in Chicago over the weekend.

One of them, Dr. Maria W. Piers, psychologist and dean of the Erikson Institute for Early Education in Chicago, said it is not television which makes young people violent, or keeps them from relating to others. It is the absence of other ingredients which make for a fulfilling life.

The other, Joseph Palombo, social worker and director of the child therapy program at the Chicago Institute for Psychoanalysis, said children's personalities are already developed before they are able to understand what is happening on the screen.

11–3 paragraph three

11–4 In the discussion of speech and meeting coverage, you learned that the when, where and how of such stories are secondary W's, and may not belong in the lead. But they usually should be near the beginning of the story, so the _____ may be a good place.

11–4 bridge

11–5 Underline the when and the how in this bridge:

More Americans are moving away from metropolitan areas than are moving to them, stirring resentment in smaller cities and rural areas "inundated" by newcomers, a population expert said Thursday.

In a report to the American Association for the Advancement of Science, Dr. Peter A. Morrison, a Rand Corp. researcher, noted that a number of cities have sought to regulate further population growth.

11–5 in a television interview yesterday

11–6 From the following bridges choose the one that includes the when, where and how elements for this story:

UNITED NATIONS (UPI) — China, in a stinging attack on the United States and the Soviet Union, has charged that the two superpowers are engaged in a fierce struggle of aggression and subversion to dominate the world.
A. The Chinese also called for the expulsion of Lon Nol's Cambodian delegates to the United Nations and the seating of representatives of Prince Norodom Sihanouk, now in exile in Peking.
B. The bulk of the attack was aimed at the Soviet Union, which was called "socialist in words, imperialist in deeds."
C. In a 40-minute address yesterday to the U.N. General Assembly, Chiao Kuan-hua, vice foreign minister of the Peking government, derided talk of a global easing of tensions.
D. The Chinese blast followed a series of diplomatic protests charging the United States and the Soviet Union with "aggression" in Africa, Asia and Latin America.

11–6 Paragraph C includes the when (yesterday), the where (before the General Assembly), and the how (in a 40-minute address).

11–7 One use of the bridge, then, is to give secondary W's not used in the _____.

11–7 lead

11–8 In most news stories, the reader must be told the source of the information. This is called *attribution*. Since attribution is important to the reader's understanding of the facts, it should be near the beginning of the story, but often not in the lead. So the bridge may be a good place for the _____.

11–8 attribution

11–9 Underline the attribution in the bridge of this story:

PORT-AU-PRINCE, Haiti (AP) — The upsurge in U.S. commodity prices is making itself felt along the food lines that help sustain thousands of needy persons here in Haiti.
"We've begun to feel it already," says Neal O'Toole, assistant director of the CARE food relief program in this Caribbean republic.
"Now there's no more milk," he shrugged. "And if you have soybean futures going up, it's going to affect the program."
CARE, which stands for the Cooperative for American Relief Everywhere, depends on American grain surpluses and an abundance of soybeans for its supplies.

11–9 says Neal O'Toole, assistant director of the CARE food relief program in this Caribbean republic.

11–10 When you learned about blind leads, you discovered that the *name* and *identification* of an unfamiliar person may be placed in the second paragraph. Thus a bridge following a blind lead should include the person's _____ and _____.

11–10 name identification

11–11 In the paragraphs that follow the lead, you may have to give some background information to help the reader understand the story.

Background often is essential so the reader will fully _____ the story.

59

11–11   understand

11–12   In which paragraph does the background information appear? _____

MEMPHIS (AP) — Court-ordered desegregation busing began today for the approximately 40,000 pupils in the Memphis public schools, one of the South's largest school systems.

A May 13 order by U.S. District Court Judge Robert M. McRae Jr. calls for 155 buses to cover 508 routes. Starting times at the 140 schools involved will be staggered so buses can make multiple runs. The busing is expected to cost $1.6 million this school year.

Officials were prepared to cope with any difficulties. Seventy tactical police were on standby to augment motorcycle officers and police helicopters assigned to busing.

11–12   paragraph two

11–13   Putting all the background in one paragraph as in 11–12 can slow the story and make it appear dull and historical. To prevent dullness due to backgrounding, try combining news and background in the bridge. Underline the news in the bridge of this story:

SACRAMENTO (AP) — The Sacramento Bee says the United States received part of its intelligence information before the ill-fated 1961 Bay of Pigs invasion of Cuba from three reputed Mafia members and an associate who had run Havana casinos.

The Bee, in a story by reporter Denny Walsh, said yesterday the CIA had promised the mobsters that for their help they would be allowed to recover $750,000 they had buried in Cuba and could reopen their casinos after Fidel Castro's downfall.

"The information they supplied to the CIA supposedly pinpointed troop and naval vessel positions," Walsh wrote.

11–13   the CIA had promised the mobsters that for their help they would be allowed to recover $750,000 they had buried in Cuba and could reopen their casinos after Fidel Castro's downfall.

11–14   Underline the news in the bridge of this story:

MIAMI (AP) — An 11-year Central Intelligence Agency employee who resigned last month says former CIA Director Richard Helms denied to agents in 1964 that the agency engaged in assassination.

In a copyright story in today's Miami Herald, Mike Ackerman said he is disappointed at the failure of the current director, William Colby, to deny the existence of such plots.

"Richard Helms, then chief of clandestine services and later director of the CIA, addressed a training class of which I was a member," said Ackerman, 34, who at the time was in training to be a clandestine agent.

11–14   Mike Ackerman said he is disappointed at the failure of the current director, William Colby, to deny the existence of such plots.

11–15   So far, we've discussed four basic functions of the bridge. Name them.

_____

_____

_____

_____

60

11–15	secondary W's attribution identification background
11–16	news
11–17	short/brief

11–16   To review, bridge paragraphs can become dull and historical. To prevent this, combine _____ and background in the bridge paragraph.

11–17   As you've learned, all paragraphs in news stories should be kept short to make reading easier. Since there are so many things that might be put in bridge paragraphs, be especially careful to keep them reasonably _____.

Chapter
TWELVE

transitions and organization

12-1   If a story is to proceed in an orderly, readable fashion from beginning to end, some system of arranging the facts and carrying the reader from one fact to another is necessary. You already have considered techniques for developing the lead and bridging paragraphs. Here are some devices to use to create a smooth, orderly flow of facts in the body of the story.

12-2   The familiar inverted pyramid concept of arranging facts in diminishing order of importance is itself an organizational device, but a complex story may have so many primary and secondary facts that additional organizing is necessary within the inverted pyramid framework.

Thus only a rather short and simple story is likely to be organized adequately using only the _____ _____.

12-2   inverted pyramid

12-3   An organizational device that can be used in moderately complex stories as a supplement to the inverted pyramid to make reading of the story easier is the *transitional paragraph:*

Among the items the commission will consider are a request for the purchase of a helicopter to be used by the county engineer for mosquito control, a proposal to establish a cemetery in a residential neighborhood and a request by the sheriff to buy an armored personnel carrier.

This paragraph groups upcoming points in a story, and prepares the reader for them. The story should next give the details in the same order as the main points appear in the transitional paragraph.

In this example, the story first should discuss the _____ _____, and it should conclude with the _____.

12-3   helicopter request
personnel carrier request

12-4   A story that quotes several sources on the same subject *could* quote first one source in full, then the next source, then the next, etc. However, this system would make it very difficult for the reader to compare the views of the sources.

A better organizational system is to group the sources' comments by *topic*. This makes it easier for the reader to _____ the views of the sources.

12-4   compare

12-5   Here's an example of a transitional paragraph in a story about the views held by two experts on automobile air pollution control devices:

Both men agreed that pollution control devices are reducing gasoline mileage, but they disagreed on how the public will react to lower mileage.

Note that the reader now knows what topic is about to be discussed, and has a general idea of the sources' views on that topic.

The next few paragraphs should give details of _____

12–5   each source's views on the topic

12–6   The transitional paragraph in frame 12–5 could be considered a broad paraphrase of the direct quotations that follow it. This technique of using a paraphrase as a transition and immediately supporting it with the direct quotation from which the paraphrase is drawn is perhaps the most basic and useful developmental device in journalistic writing. Consider this simple example:

> Dr. Jones said he is unable to give up smoking, despite repeated attempts.
>
> "I know smoking will be the death of me, but I just don't have the backbone to quit. Lord knows I've tried," he said.

This example uses a _____ as a transition, and then supports it with a _____ _____.

12–6   paraphrase direct quotation

12–7   Even a rather long and complex story can be developed smoothly by alternating paraphrases and supporting direct quotes. Note how the technique is used in the following example:

> TALLAHASSEE (AP) — The all-male House Rules Committee, unwilling to alienate either faction of the opposite sex and uncertain how the votes stacked up, yesterday put off a showdown on women's rights.
>
> In an unrecorded voice vote, the committee adopted an apparently prearranged motion by Rep. Carl Ogden, D-Jacksonville, postponing a vote on the sexual equality amendment to the U.S. Constitution.
>
> **OGDEN said later supporters of the amendment were uncertain they had the votes for committee approval of the ratification resolution.**
>
> "I saw no reason if we were going to lose the bill of putting anyone out on the hook for it or against it," Ogden said.
>
> **The delay was neither a surprise nor a disappointment to Rep. Jane Robinson, one of five house members who urged the committee to put the amendment before the house.**
>
> "I have lived with men for 46 years and this is a typical male escape hatch," Mrs. Robinson said.
>
> **SHE ADDED**, however, "I don't much blame them for not wanting to do it today."
>
> **Two groups of 100 women, and a handful of men supporters, put the committee on the spot during a two-hour hearing with impassioned arguments for and against the women's rights amendment.**
>
> Patricia Dore, a Florida State University assistant law professor argued that the amendment "will not destroy the family unit, nor will it degrade the role of wife and mother."
>
> But Mrs. Rex Reed of Jacksonville, representing 32 women's clubs, contended that Equal Rights Amendment proponents "desire to deprive the majority of women of their God-given rights to be wives and mothers, driving them into the job market and forcing their children into day care centers run by the federal government."
>
> "MAN HAS given woman his heart, his name and his money," Mrs. Reed said. "What more could she possibly want?"
>
> **The draft was another hotly controversial issue, with supporters of the amendment conceding women would be subject to military service but contending they could not get combat duty.**
>
> "I say as an ex-Marine I don't see the horror of military service for women," said Maxine MacKay, a University of South Florida professor. "I don't see them slogging through rice paddies in mud and blood carrying an M1 rifle."
>
> Louis Putney, a Tampa attorney, said "if we go into another war, which we're almost bound to someday, we men of this country will be sitting at

home sending our women, our daughters and our granddaughters overseas to fight our war."

12–8   A useful but somewhat specialized organizational technique is the listing in *separate paragraphs* of the points the story will cover.

The list of points gets extra emphasis by the use of _____ paragraphs.

12–8   separate

12–9   Some papers introduce each paragraph in such a list with a number, whereas others use a *bullet,* which is a large dot to the left of the item. When typing a story, use an asterisk for a bullet. Here's an example:

The commission also was asked:
*To appoint a new county administrator;
*To increase the county budget for health services;
*To establish branch health offices in rural areas.

These points could have been listed in a single paragraph, but the use of separate paragraphs and bullets gives the points extra _____.

12–9   emphasis

12–10   Whether a list is one paragraph or several, make all verb forms *parallel*. In the example in frame 12–9, all the verbs are in the infinitive form — *to appoint, to increase, to establish*

Gerunds — *appointing, increasing, establishing* — might also have been used in 12–9. However, never mix gerunds and infinitives because they are not _____ verb forms.

12–10   parallel

12–11   Even when the basic structure of the story has been determined, the use of key *words or phrases of transition* can do much to smooth the flow of the story.

You've already considered the use of story organization and paragraphs of transition to smooth story development. But you should know that _____ and _____ can also smooth story development.

12–11   words   phrases

12–12   Here are a few words and phrases of transition and what they can do for your story:

Indicate additional information: also, besides, and, again, in addition

Indicate time relationships: later, soon, before, after, afterward, earlier, previously, meanwhile, simultaneously, next, finally

Indicate comparisons and contrasts: similarly, like,

answers

1. bridge/second paragraph
2. name   identification
3. news
4. name   background
5. B
6. paraphrase
7. paragraphs   bullets

Chapter
THIRTEEN

quotations and paraphrases

13–1   You have already learned to eliminate unnecessary words and to write as directly as possible. Unfortunately, you will receive much valuable information buried under wasted words, and you will face the problem of keeping your story crisp and precise, yet capturing all the information.

When faced with an unnecessarily long quotation, paraphrase the quotation by extracting relevant information and putting it in your own words.

Thus, to put the source's meaning into your own words is to

_____ the quotation.

13–1   paraphrase

13–2   Here's a statement from Joe Jones:

"I think I have made clear that no reasonable person could have approved of the behavior of our college students last year, but I detect indications that their conduct is somewhat improved this year."

Which of the following is a paraphrase of what Jones said? _____

> A. Jones is an outspoken but somewhat optimistic critic of student conduct.
>
> B. Jones disapproved of student conduct last year, but said conduct this year is better.

13–2   Sentence B is the paraphrase. The essence of what Jones said remains, but unneeded words have been trimmed. Sentence A subjectively evaluates rather than restates the quote.

13–3   A paraphrase must be an accurate restatement. Here's a statement from Jim Smith:

"Although the mayor's proposal has been generally well received, I think it's by no means perfect. Much, if not most, of the enthusiasm we've seen so far may prove to be premature."

Which of the following sentences does *not* paraphrase Smith's statement accurately? _____

> A. Smith said he opposes the mayor's proposal, in spite of its generally favorable reception.
>
> B. Smith said he thinks the mayor's proposal has faults, in spite of its generally favorable reception.

13–3   Sentence A is not accurate. Smith may be willing to support the proposal even though he sees problems with it. He did *not* say he opposed it.

13–4   When paraphrasing a statement, be especially careful not to give a cause-and-effect relationship if no such relationship exists. Look at the following statement from Professor John Anderson:

"I received a letter from the student in which she requested that she be given a passing grade, noted several inconsistencies in my grading policy and reminded me that her father was a fraternity brother of mine. I have given the situation much thought and have decided that the student will pass."

Which of the following more accurately paraphrases the professor?

_____

70

A. Anderson said he decided the student would pass after receiving a reminder that her father had been in his fraternity.

B. Anderson said he decided the student would pass after receiving a letter from her.

13–4 Sentence B is a better paraphrase. Although some details have been omitted, the paraphrase does not mislead; sentence A clearly implies that Professor John Anderson decided to give the student a passing grade *because* her father belonged to the professor's fraternity.

13–5 partial

13–6 gibbering of fools

13–5 Occasionally, a quotable word or phrase may be buried in a sentence that is too long to quote in full. In such a case, quote just the strong *part*, and paraphrase the rest. This is called a _____ quote.

13–6 Underline the part of Judge George Johnson's statement that is most quotable and could be used in a partial quote:

"Reports that I intend to resign from the bench and run for governor are incorrect and should be disregarded as the gibbering of fools."

13–7 Here's how the partial quote from frame 13–6 might look in a sentence:

Johnson denied reports he plans to run for governor, and called them the "gibbering of fools."

13–8 A football coach made this comment about his team's next game:

"State's cow college image is certainly misleading. They're strong, but they could easily lull an opponent into underestimating their potential for playing high-quality ball."

Which of the following sentences shows the most effective use of a partial quote? _____

A. The coach denied that State would be a weak opponent, and said they could "easily lull" an opponent into underestimating them.

B. The coach said State would not be a weak opponent, and added that they have the "potential" for playing well.

C. The coach denied that State would be a weak opponent, and said their "cow college image" is misleading.

13–8 In A, "easily lull" is a weak quote; neither the meaning nor the wording is especially quotable. In B, "potential" might be a possibility if the coach was implying more than his words said — if he implied clearly that their potential wouldn't be realized, for example. There are better partial quotes in this case. The best choice is C. "Cow college image" is a vivid expression and is central to the coach's point.

13–9 which we've had for 60 years

13–10 three periods

13–11 an ellipsis (three periods) plus the period to end the sentence

13–12 a comma

13–13 paraphrase   partial quote

13–9 When part of a quotation is weak, that part may be omitted. Such an omission is called an *ellipsis*. Underline the weak phrase in this quotation:

"If any more of our football players get hurt, we'll have to change the school colors, which we've had for 60 years, from white and blue to black and blue."

13–10 Three periods (. . .) signal an ellipsis. In the example in frame 13–9, the phrase "which we've had for 60 years" would be replaced in the copy by _____.

13–11 An ellipsis can indicate omitted words at the beginning, middle or end of a sentence. But if an ellipsis comes at the end of a sentence a period must follow it:

"In life, the most enjoyable experiences are rarely the most instructive . . . ."

In the example, the four periods indicate _____.

13–12 When grammar or readability requires it, a comma, question mark or other punctuation is placed before the ellipsis.

In the following quotation, what punctuation should precede the ellipsis? _____

"I hate to be critical of a man whom I've considered to be a friend of mine . . . but a terrible error has been made."

13–13 The ellipsis is seldom used, and may look stilted or confuse some readers. Use it only if you are sure that the quote is improved by it and that no other form of quotation is better.

To review, the forms of quotation discussed before the ellipsis were the _____ and the _____.

13–14 The last form of quotation is the *direct quote* — the source's *exact words*. An effective direct quote is brief, vivid and in context. Read the following statement:

"The concept of a museum as a graveyard for the corpse of man's past is outmoded. There's no longer any excuse for expecting people to flock to a place where they wander down aisles, stare at dusty bones and rocks in dusty display cases, go home tired and footsore, and end up getting no more out of it than they could have had by looking at pictures in their living rooms. We think museums should allow people to actually experience elements of man's history."

Is the following an effective, direct quote? _____

"Museums should allow people to experience elements of man's history."

13–14 No. The exact words of the source have not been used. The passage would have to be presented as a paraphrase without quotation marks.

13–15 Is the following an effective, direct quote from the statement in frame 13–14? _____

"There's no longer any excuse for expecting people to flock to a place where they wander down aisles, stare at dusty bones and rocks in dusty display cases, go home tired and footsore, and end up getting no more out of it than they could have had by looking at pictures in their living rooms."

13–15 No. It's just too long. A paraphrase would have been better. For example: People should get more from visiting a museum than from looking at pictures.

13–16 One last example. Is the following an effective, direct quote from the statement in frame 13–14? _____

"The concept of a museum as a graveyard for the corpse of man's past is outmoded."

13–16 Yes. Consider the elements of a good direct quote. It's entirely in the source's words, it's brief, it's vivid and it's in context.

13–17 In using quotations, avoid the overuse of any one quote form. Although a paraphrase should carry the bulk of the information, carefully chosen partial and direct quotes will add life and interest to the story.

So a well-developed story will consist of a _____ of the various forms of quotation.

13–17 variety/combination

13–18 When giving the source or *attribution* (who said it) for your news facts, the word *said* is the best verb to use. Don't strain for synonyms; the verb _____ is the best one to use when attributing information.

13–18 said

13–19 In your first newswriting course, use *said* for most attribution because it is neutral in connotation. Possible synonyms, such as *claimed, charged, advocated* and *denied,* are not _____ in connotation.

13–19 neutral

13–20 Notice that *said* is used extensively in this story:

NEW YORK (AP) — General Electric said Sunday it has developed a new battery for heart pacemakers that should last as long as the predicted life of nuclear pacemakers at "a fraction" of the cost.

GE said chemically powered batteries — not the nuclear-powered pacemakers now being evaluated in a number of patients — will prove to be the ultimate answer to long life heart pacemakers.

The new battery, a sodium battery, is smaller and lighter than the mercury zinc chemical battery now in wide use and should last much longer, GE said.

GE said its batteries are scheduled to be implanted in human patients within two years. They are being tested in animals now at GE's Medical Systems Business Division in Milwaukee.

Dr. Arthur M. Bueche of the GE Research and Development Center in Schenectady, N.Y., said the sodium-bromine batteries should provide a pacemaker with 10 years of continuous operation.

A 10-year life span is now predicted for the nuclear-powered pacemaker, GE said, at a cost of $4,800. GE did not give a specific price for its product.

Conventional pacemakers must be replaced by surgery every 24 to 28 months, GE said. They cost about $1,000 to $1,500, according to the company.

13–21   Beginning newswriters sometimes err by tying themselves to the chronology of the speech or event they are covering with phrases such as, "Jones began by noting . . ." or "In conclusion, he said . . . ."

Effective news story development seldom follows the chronology of a news event. Reporters should avoid words such as *began* or

_____ .

13–21   concluded

13–22   Occasionally, the use of verbs of attribution such as *stated* or *added* may be appropriate. *Stated* is rather formal, and should be used only if a formal (probably written) statement is being quoted. *Added* is somewhat like *in conclusion* because it dictates the order the facts in the story must follow. But, if a quotation is indeed an afterthought, the use of *added* is correct.

Before selecting a specialized verb of attribution, be sure the circumstances make that verb the most _____ one to use.

13–22   appropriate

13–23   Editors differ over the use of *according to* in expressing attribution. Some argue that *according to* implies doubt, just as the word *claimed* does. Some say it is unnecessarily long and should be avoided. Others contend *according to* is a reasonably neutral alternative to *said* and can be used for variety or readability.

In general, however, the verb of attribution that beginning newswriters should use most of the time is _____.

13–23   said

13–24   Although attribution in the present tense *(he says)* is used effectively in some feature stories, timeliness and the changing nature of news developments make the past tense *(he said)* most appropriate for new stories.

If a reporter interviews a source Monday afternoon and the interview doesn't appear in the newspaper until Tuesday afternoon, what the source *says* on Tuesday may be very different from what he _____ on Monday.

13–24   said

13–25   Normally, it's important for the *name* of the source to appear in the story, so the reader can weigh the source's credibility. The

74

practice of printing the source's name also discourages irresponsible statements. Be wary if a source asks you not to print his _____.

13–25 name

13–26 Infrequently, you may decide the source's name should not be used (for instance, when it might jeopardize the source's job). In such a case, use the most precise *indirect* identification possible without identifying the source.

Which of these indirect identifications is the most *precise?* _____

    A. *a source in the mayor's office*

    B. *a city employee*

    C. *an informed source*

    D. *mayor's secretary*

13–26 D is the most precise, but it might identify the source (there may be only one secretary). The phrase in A is probably best.

13–27 Omitting a source's name is, however, rarely justified. Keep in mind that some sources hope to use the story to damage someone without taking the responsibility.

So, especially before using information without giving the source's name, double and triple check the information to be sure it is

_____.

13–27 accurate/true

13–28 Assume now that you have a story with only one source, and that the source has been fully identified. In placing attribution in the body of this story, you could locate it at the beginning, middle or end of the information. Look at this example:

> The 36th Street bridge over the Rock River is a "death trap" and will kill an average of 10 persons a year until it is replaced, according to Public Safety Director Thomas Adams.
> Adams told the city commission last night that the bridge, constructed in 1949, is the site of more accidents than any other location in the city.
> "For the last six years, an average of 10 persons per year have died on that bridge, and I have no doubt that rate will continue," Adams said.
> "Despite repeated requests that the 36th Street death trap be given highest priority in our road construction program, this commission has ignored the problem," Adams said. "It's time now that you take action."
> The city commission has concentrated on street improvements in the downtown business district in response to pressure by businessmen, and the question of public safety has been ignored, Adams said.

Note that most of the attribution comes at the _____ of the information.

13–28 end

13–29 The end of the phrase or statement is the usual and most desirable place for attribution in a story with a single source, since it indicates the source, yet keeps the focus of attention on the information itself.

13–30 When you have several sources, and change from one to another in the body of the story, each new attribution must be at the *beginning* of the information so the reader can see immediately that the source has changed. Underline the new attribution showing a change in source in the following example:

> The grading policies were far from arbitrary, and had been developed during his 35 years as a college professor, Jones said.
> Student spokesman Andrew Smith said, however, requests by students during the term to check their grades and discuss their progress had been refused.

13–30   student spokesman Andrew Smith said

13–31   In stories with more than one source, it's very confusing when attribution is not perfectly clear. So, careful attribution is especially vital in stories that have _____.

13–31   more than one source

13–32   Placement of attribution in the middle of a quote can sometimes be effective, but it must be done carefully and sparingly. Look at this effective example:

> "This committee has called me a perjurer," Thompson said, "and I am entitled to an apology."

This "splitting" of a quote with attribution is effective because the attribution falls in a natural pause in the quote and can be read smoothly.

What's wrong with the following placement of the attribution?

> "This committee," Thompson said, "has called me a perjurer, and I am entitled to an apology."

13–32   Not smooth; the attribution is not in a natural pause.

13–33   Another objection to placing attribution in the middle of a quote, is that the attribution breaks the reader's train of thought, making understanding the quote itself more difficult.

Examine the following example from a single-source story.

> "Of the nine boys originally arrested following the offense, four were released without being charged, but spent a night in jail. Charges on two other boys were dropped but three will be charged as adults and will appear in court tomorrow."

In this example, the attribution should go _____.

13–33   At the end; at the start would be good, too. Placing the attribution in the middle would confuse the reader.

13–34   Punctuation and capitalization of quotations in journalistic writing follow most of the usual grammatical rules. For example, quotation marks (" ") should enclose only the exact words of the source. If you aren't sure you have the source's _____ words, use a paraphrase; do not use quotation marks.

13–34   exact

13–35   The attribution of a direct quotation should always be set off from the quotation by a comma.

Regardless of whether the attribution comes before or after a direct quotation, it should always be set off by a _____.

13–35 comma

13–36 When attribution comes *before* a paraphrase, no comma is needed. Is the following paraphrase punctuated correctly? _____

Thompson said his office is so small two people can't sit down in it at the same time.

13–36 Yes, the paraphrase is punctuated correctly.

13–37 When attribution comes *after* a paraphrase, a comma must be used. Is this paraphrase punctuated correctly? _____

Thompson tends to exaggerate about his office Smith said.

13–37 No. A comma belongs before the attribution, "Smith said."

13–38 When a complete sentence is quoted directly, it must begin with a capital letter. A partial quotation should not be capitalized unless it begins with a proper noun.

Even when used as a direct quote, a complete sentence must begin with a _____ _____.

13–38 capital letter

13–39 In journalistic style, commas and periods at the end of direct quotations are placed inside the quotation marks.

Which of the following examples is *incorrectly* punctuated?

_____

A. "Your spelling is abysmal," he said.
B. He said, "Your grammar also leaves much to be desired."
C. "I'd like to drop the course", the student said.

13–39 C is incorrect. The comma is outside the quotation marks.

13–40 When the entire quotation forms a question, the question mark is placed inside the quotation marks and the comma is omitted. Look at the following example:

"Have they left the house yet?" he asked.

In the example, the entire quotation forms a question and the question mark is placed _____ the quotation marks.

13–40 inside

13–41 When the quotation comes at the end of a question, the question mark is placed *outside* the quotation marks, as in the following example:

How could his colleagues have named him as "outstanding"?

In this example the quotation is at the end of a question, so the question mark is placed _____ the quotation marks.

13–41 outside

13–42 Single quotes (' ') are uncommon in journalistic writing, but they are necessary whenever there is a quotation within a quotation, or whenever quotation marks are needed inside another quotation.

Look at the following example:

"Even on national television, he referred to his opponent as 'the village idiot,'" Smith said.

In the example, *the village idiot* is a quotation within a quotation, so it is enclosed in _____ _____.

13-42 single quotes

13-43 Infrequently, the reporter may decide to quote directly a series of paragraphs without using unquoted material to break the series. In such a case, each paragraph begins with quotation marks, but only the last paragraph has closing quotation marks:

"Xxxxxxxx xxxxx xxxx xxxxxxxx xxxx xxx x xxxx xxx xx xx xxxx xxx xxx xxxxxx.

"Xxx xxxx xxx xxx xxxxxxxx x xx xx x x xxxx xxxxxxxxxx x x xxx x xx xxx xxx.

"Xxxxxxxx x xx xxxxxxx xxx x xx x xxxxx xx xxxx xxxxxx x xxx x xxxxx x xxx xxxx."

Assuming the example is an unbroken series of direct quotations, only the last paragraph has

_____ _____ _____.

13-43 closing quotation marks

13-44 A common error in quotation is the use of I, me, we, our, my, and similar personal pronouns in paraphrases. These can appear *only* in *direct quotes* in which the source refers to himself. When used in paraphrases, they appear to refer to the reporter or his newspaper and are extremely confusing to the reader.

To whom does the "we" in the following paraphrase from a newspaper story appear to refer?

Jones said that despite a persistent rumor, we have no plans to dismiss the professor.

13-44 While confusing, the "we" seems to refer to the newspaper staff.

13-45 The problem of confusing personal pronouns can be avoided in two ways. One is by using a direct or partial quote instead of a paraphrase.

To whom does the "we" in the following direct quote refer?

Jones said, "Despite a persistent rumor, we have no plans to dismiss the professor."

13-45 The "we" now appears to refer to Jones and his colleagues.

13-46 The other solution is to substitute he, she, they, their, or similar pronouns in the paraphrase of the direct quotation.

To whom does the "they" in the following paraphrase refer?

Jones said that despite a persistent rumor they have no plans to dismiss the professor.

13-46 Again, the "they" appears to refer to Jones and his colleagues.

review test for chapter 13

1. To shorten a long direct quotation without changing its meaning, you may _____ the quotation.

2. Read the following quotation:

   "An effective reporter, whether a rank beginner or an experienced veteran, should strive for brevity in his technique without sacrificing accuracy," Thomas said.

   Paraphrase Thomas' quotation _____.

3. When a quotable word or phrase appears in a longer statement, a reporter may use a paraphrase and a _____ quote in writing his or her story.

4. When you omit just a word or a phrase of a direct quotation, the omission is called an _____.

5. Such an omission is designated by _____.

6. In choosing among paraphrases, partial quotations and ellipses, remember that _____ may appear stilted and should be used sparingly.

7. An effective direct quote should be in the source's exact words, brief, vivid and _____.

8. Personal pronouns such as *I, me, we, our* and *my* should appear only in _____ quotes in which the source refers to himself.

9. Because it is neutral in connotation, the verb _____ should be used for most attribution.

10. The most desirable place for the attribution in a one-source story is at the _____ (beginning/middle/end) of a quotation.

11. Read this example:

"It's mightly unusual for an amateur golfer to thrash the professionals like that" he said.

What punctuation is needed? _____

12. In which of the following sentences is the comma correctly placed? _____

    A. "I'm overjoyed to see you," she said.

    B. "I didn't know you'd be here", he said.

    C. She said, it was a dull party.

answers

1. paraphrase
2. Reporters should try to write briefly and accurately, Thomas said.
3. partial
4. ellipsis
5. three periods
6. ellipses
7. in context
8. direct
9. said
10. end
11. a comma
12. A

Chapter FOURTEEN

sources, ethics and the law

14-1 The problem of how and when to quote is one of the most complex ethical and practical questions facing reporters. A detailed discussion is impossible here, but some general guidelines on several central issues will be given. Among these issues are on- and off-the-record and background statements.

On-the-record statements are those made by a source who knows that what he says may be published. The restraints on the reporter are his knowledge of the laws of libel and invasion of privacy, and his judgment of what is newsworthy.

Since the decision of what shall or shall not be published thus rests with the reporter rather than with the source, _____ statements are most desirable.

14-1   on-the-record

14-2 Occasionally a source will ask that something he or she is about to say be *off the record,* meaning it is not for publication. The reporter who agrees to hear an off-the-record statement is *ethically bound not to publish it*. Publication of an off-the-record statement shows a reporter to be untrustworthy and it would damage the reporter's relationship with news sources.

So, the reporter who receives information off the record (which he or she is *legally* entitled to publish) _____ (should/should not) publish it.

14-2   should not

14-3 Sources may seek to go off the record for good reasons, such as to protect the name of an innocent individual, or for bad reasons, such as to obscure improper conduct. The reporter should insist on hearing the source's reasons for wanting to go off the record *before* allowing the source to go off the record.

If the source is allowed to determine what will not appear in print, he's making a news judgment that properly should be made by the _____ .

14-3   reporter

14-4 Occasionally, after hearing an off-the-record statement, a reporter may decide that its importance is such that it should be printed. Yet, he's bound by his agreement not to use it. In such a case, the reporter's first response may be to attempt to persuade the source that the off-the-record statement should be printed.

So, when valuable information is presented off the record, the reporter's first response may be to persuade the source to put the information _____ the record.

14-4   on

14-5 If a source declines to give information on the record, the reporter may consider hearing the information off the record, then finding another source who will allow himself to be quoted.

83

Though the off-the-record information may be useful in dealing with the second source, the reporter should be careful not to _____ his first source in his story or to other sources.

14–5 identify/name

14–6 A source's desire to go off the record may make the reporter's job more difficult, but it should not keep the reporter from getting a valuable story. To sum up, the reporter should

1. Attempt to keep the source on the record
2. Try to get the source back on the record if he leaves it
3. Seek a second source

If all attempts to get on-the-record information from a source fail, the reporter's last resort is to _____.

14–6 seek a second source

14–7 Without looking back now, give the three basic approaches a reporter should take when a source attempts to go off the record:

_____

_____

_____

14–7 Keep the source on the record. Get the source back on the record. Seek a second source.

14–8 A source may insist on giving information "for background only." What this usually means is that the reporter can print the information but may not identify the source or the source's organization in any way.

As we discussed earlier, anonymous or indirectly attributed information may be inaccurate, and the reporter should check the information especially carefully to be sure it is _____.

14–8 true/accurate

14–9 As with off-the-record statements, the reporter should be reluctant to accept statements "for background only," and should try to (1) persuade the source to permit his name to be used, or (2) find a second source whose name can be used.

Both background and off-the-record statements may be inaccurate and are undesirable for publication. The reporter should try to keep all statements _____ the record.

14–9 on

14–10 While most information which appears in news stories should be attributed clearly to a source, information *of general*

84

knowledge or *readily verified fact* usually does not require attribution. Which of the following statements do not require attribution? _____

    A.   It rained here yesterday.

    B.   The capital of New Jersey is Trenton.

    C.   After the fall of Constantinople to the Turks in 1453, Greece became part of the Ottoman Empire.

    D.   Conventions generated more than $2.6 million in retail sales in the city last year.

14–10   A, B, C

14–11   Attribution of old information can sometimes give the misleading impression that a change of some sort has occurred. For example,

> An amount equal to 55 percent of the total tangible taxes collected by the state is to be distributed to the counties through revenue sharing, State Attorney General Carl January said today.

If this revenue sharing formula has been in effect for several years, the attribution should not be used because it is _____.

14–11   old information (misleading, confusing)

14–12   Under some circumstances, such as when dealing with opinion or controversy, the reporter should be especially careful to ensure that the source of his information is clearly given. Note this example:

> Construction of an attractive pedestrian mall and a complete ban on cars in the downtown area would lure shoppers back from the suburbs, City Planning Director Lewis Smith said yesterday.
> The pleasant novelty of shopping in an area of trees and greenery rather than sheets of asphalt would be irresistible.

Because the second paragraph is opinion rather than general knowledge or verifiable fact, the _____ of the information must be given.

14–12   source

14–13   Careful attribution especially is needed when a source makes a prediction on a matter while debate or official action is still underway. For example,

> A new 42-store shopping center east of the Leesburg city limits will have its grand opening by next fall.
> Final site approval by the county commission is expected Tuesday, developer Carl M. Wilson said.

Since the county commission could refuse or delay final approval, the lead should include careful _____.

14–13   attribution

14–14   Whatever compromises a newswriter is forced to make because of the pressure of time, or for any other reason, factual accuracy must not be compromised.

Perhaps the most important minutes spent on any story are those used for double and triple checking trouble spots such as street addresses, dates, titles and spelling of proper names of people, organizations, places and things, so the writer can be positive they are _____ .

14–14   accurate/correct

14–15   A newspaper's credibility is its most valuable possession, and one that is easily lost. A beginning reporter may see little damage in spelling Joe Smithe's name as Smith, but many readers may spot the error and wonder if a paper that errs on the small, simple matters can be trusted on major issues.

Likewise, a reader who drives across town to arrive at a meeting on Wednesday at 7 p.m., the time and day reported by the paper, and finds that the meeting is scheduled for Thursday at 7 p.m., will lose a great deal of _____ in the paper.

14–15   trust/faith

14–16   Factual inaccuracy also carries the risk of legal action against the reporter and his newspaper.
For instance, police might say a local man named Jim Anderson was arrested for public intoxication. A reporter might find a J. L. Anderson of 210 N. Elm St. listed in the telephone directory, assume he's the man the police arrested, and use his name and address in a story of the arrest. But if J. L. Anderson turns out to be Jason Anderson, and is *not* the man arrested, the reporter and his newspaper may very well become defendants in a libel suit.

Thus the reporter may learn the hard way that to falsely impute illegal or antisocial actions such as drunkenness to a person of good reputation is a form of factual inaccuracy that can lead to a successful suit for _____ .

14–16   libel

14–17   Libel is a printed or broadcast statement or picture that causes public hatred, contempt or ridicule of a person or group of persons, or that hurts his/their business, profession or livelihood.

Exactly what may be libelous varies with time, place and circumstances, but there is always danger in printing or broadcasting material by which the reputation or livelihood of a person or persons can be _____ .

14–17   damaged/injured

14–18   There are four broad categories of libelous statements:

1. Imputing the commission of a crime or antisocial act (as was done earlier in the example of Anderson).

2.   Imputing a lack of integrity.

3.   Damaging a person's occupational standing or ability to earn a living.

4.   Imputing insanity or a contagious disease.

A statement may not be obviously libelous, but it may nonetheless lead to a successful suit. For example, if an error in addresses in a story seems to indicate that a single man and a single woman are living together, a successful libel suit might ensue. Of the four categories, this example is covered in number _____.

14–18 two — and possibly one and three as well

14–19   Libel actions can result from careless "labeling" of groups and individuals. Dangerous defamatory labels include *liar, thief, crook, fraud, imposter, criminal, racketeer, swindler* and *traitor*.

Defamatory labels often appear in headlines or in blind leads, where proper names are not used immediately. Note this dangerous attempt to brighten up an arrest story.

A local con man found himself in city jail yesterday after he attempted to sell a stolen car to a police detective.
The man, Joseph Q. Smith, 1301 Dakota Ave., approached Detective Allan White . . .

If Smith was found innocent of the charges and sued for libel, the basis of the suit could be the defamatory label _____.

14–19   con man

14–20   Here's another example. Assume you're a professional journalist and a rival publication prints a story calling you a *libel vendor*.

Recall the four broad categories of libel. The term may be libelous because it _____ .

14–20 damages your occupational standing and your ability to earn a living

14–21   Some specialized forms of reporting such as reviews of books, movies, works of art and athletic events as well as coverage of certain legal and governmental subjects have partial protection against libel judgments, but the best general safeguard is *accuracy*. As a practical matter, the *truth* or *accuracy* of a story is virtually a complete defense in court.

So, both to maintain reader confidence in the newspaper and to guard against libel judgments, the reporter must do everything possible to be sure that every statement of fact in his story is _____.

14–21   accurate

14–22   In attempting to establish the accuracy of a statement as a defense in a libel suit, it is *not* sufficient to show that you accurately quoted information you were given. You must show that the substance of the quote itself is accurate.

For instance, assume Mr. A. has been quoted as saying that Mr. B has served a prison sentence. If Mr. B sues you for libel, you must prove that he has indeed served a prison sentence — not simply that you accurately quoted Mr. A's erroneous statement.

Even when information comes to you from another person, you as the reporter are still responsible for being sure the information is

_____.

14–22   true

14–23   A compulsion to verify information from every source is a healthy quality in a journalist. The impressive, gray-haired clerk of courts who solemnly assures you he remembers the defendant's name could be wrong — and could turn you into a defendant yourself. Printed sources contain typographical errors and become outdated. Your own memory is faulty. Double and triple check the facts.

If several independent sources agree, the chance of error can be reduced. So the reporter should not hesitate to double and _____ check his facts.

14–23   triple

1. If a source wants to tell a reporter something that is not for publication, the source may say the information is

   _____ _____ _____.

2. When a source who has important information attempts to go off the record, the reporter's three basic approaches are

   A. To try to keep the source on the record.

   B. _____

   C. _____

3. Occasionally a source will be willing to give information for background only. This means the information can be printed but the source cannot be _____.

4. One reason for accuracy in reporting all facts is the possible loss of reader _____.

5. A second reason for accuracy in reporting is to help guard against lawsuits for _____.

6. Special efforts for accuracy are necessary whenever the reporter deals with material that could damage a person's

   _____ or _____.

7. Look at the following example:

   > A jolly drunk found an unappreciative audience last night when he stumbled into Central Police Headquarters and treated officers to his rendition of "Home on the Range."
   > Police charged the vocalist, James T. Olson, with public intoxication and . . . .

   After Olson proves in court that he simply was having a reaction to a prescription medication he was taking, the reporter may be named in a libel suit because of the defamatory label

   _____.

answers

1. off the record
2. B. To try to get the source back on the record.
   C. To seek a second source.
3. named/identified
4. confidence/faith/trust
5. libel
6. reputation livelihood
7. jolly drunk

Chapter
FIFTEEN

writing

15-1   Human interest elements were discussed in Chapter 1. Review the types of human interest and look over the story examples in 1–10 through 1–20.

15-2   Even though you may be covering a routine news event, if there is a good _____ _____ angle, then that angle generally should be given strong emphasis.

15-2   human interest

15-3   This kind of story is called a *news feature*, because the story is based on a timely event or occurrence. The reporter may have begun on a _____ story assignment, but he or she will emphasize human interest and the end product will be a news feature.

15-3   news

15-4   The reporter has to determine how to handle each story assignment. When there is little or no human interest, the reporter may write a straight news story. When there is human interest, the reporter may write a _____ _____.

15-4   news feature

15-5   The purpose of the news story is to inform, whereas the purpose of the feature story is to entertain. The news feature includes elements of both types of stories.
    How much of each is blended in the news feature depends on the story situation. The writer generally has to decide which function will be dominant — information or entertainment — and then write the story accordingly.

    The story situation, then, usually dictates what the main function of the story will be — to _____ or to _____.

15-5   inform   entertain

15-6   One news feature begins with three paragraphs of human interest; the remainder of the story is pure information. The primary purpose of this story would be to _____.

    Another story is based on a timely event or situation, but is almost pure human interest. The primary purpose of this story would be to

_____.

15-6   inform entertain

15-7   Read both news feature examples:

A. BERKELEY, Calif. (UPI) — A massage parlor employee didn't let the fact that he was nude stop him from chasing three armed robbers down the street.
    Police said that the men forced three male and three female employees of the Xanadu massage parlor to strip and then took $800.
    One victim, Robert N. Greene, 33, noticed one of the bandits dropped a pistol and grabbed it. He pulled the trigger twice but it failed to discharge.

The robbers took off down a street and Greene — still unclothed — followed. He again pulled the trigger, and this time it discharged. But the robbers were not hit, and they made good their escape.

B. WASHINGTON (UPI) — Sixty years after it chugged off into oblivion, the steam-powered automobile may be tuning up for a comeback.

If the country gets really serious about licking air pollution, says Resources for the Future Inc., it might take a look at modern-day versions of the Stanley Steamer, the White and the Locomobile.

From all standpoints of technology, "an acceptable steam powered automobile could be put on the road in a very few years," said a special study published in RFF's annual report.

Electric autos also would help the smog problem, the report said, but would need "a decade or so" of development to become high performance vehicles matching gasoline-fueled internal combustion engines.

Story A's main function is _____ (information/entertainment).

Story B's main function is _____ (information/entertainment).

15–7 entertainment
information

15–8 News features may be planned in advance when a reporter or editor anticipates a human interest angle of a story. But news features often result when least expected from routine events and situations.

Which of these two news features reports an event that occurred unexpectedly? _____

A. Ben Raymond is a farmer turned preacher who wants to study the Bible. But he can't read, so at the age of 110 he's returned to school.

Raymond is enrolled at the Orange County Adult Reading Academy, hoping to improve his reading.

A farmer for most of his years, he never attended school. Wednesday he walked in grinning, leaning slightly on a wooden cane he carved himself.

He sat down at a table like someone convinced he was going to enjoy his first day at school.

B. MIAMI (AP) — In his rush to answer an old woman's screams for help, Hector Tapanes left his apartment door unlocked. When he returned home from his good deed, $1,200 was missing.

Police said Tapanes, 32, responded to the screams of Blanca Galinda, an 87-year-old widowed grandmother, after two young thieves tore a gold chain, cross and religious medal from her throat and ran.

He caught the thieves, recovered the stolen property and made a full report to the arresting police he had summoned.

After Tapanes returned home, he discovered that $1,200 in rents from the apartment house he manages was missing.

15–8 B

15–9 A second kind of feature is the *feature story*, sometimes called a *straight feature*. Unlike the news feature, it is seldom tied directly with a timely event or occurrence.

The feature story is seldom dependent on _____ as is the news feature.

93

15–9   timeliness

15–10   There is a saying that there aren't any dull subjects, just dull writers. With the feature story, almost any topic can make an interesting story if it is well written.

Almost any topic can make a good feature story if it is written so that it will _____ the reader.

15–10   interest

15–11   People, places and things are feature topics.

Persons in the public eye are frequently subjects of features. There are also "little people" stories, about persons not in the limelight who have interesting stories to tell.

Places and things as feature topics also range from the well known to the little known. Like prominent persons, well-known places and things usually have built-in reader interest.

Stories about little-known places and things usually require some kind of angle, such as the unusual, in order to capture _____ interest.

15–11   reader

15–12   An example of a feature on a little-known place is a story on a small Florida town. The beginning:

Beneath a canopy of moss-draped oaks, Windsor sleeps in the midsummer heat and dreams of the past. Huge old Victorian homes, some ramshackle, others gutted and padlocked, stand along State Road 325, just 10 miles from Gainesville, their windowpanes like blank eyes in the early morning sun.

Few cars pass now, but back in 1890 the roadway bustled with traffic, both stylish buggies and wagons hauling citrus, the fruit of life for Windsor.

The story angle, or dominant element, was that a freeze killed the citrus trees, resulting in the town's decline. The headline: "Windsor's Dreams Were Frozen in 1895."

15–13   Although well-known-place feature stories may have a main angle, many — such as travel articles and features about well-known cities — don't.

Little-known-place stories, however, usually require some kind of _____ to gain reader interest.

15–13   angle

15–14   Few of the conventions used in writing the news story apply to the feature. Those that do apply are essentially the criteria of any good writing — clarity, conciseness and directness.

The style and form of the feature story are quite _____ from those of the news story.

15–14   different

15–15   There are no rules for the style and form of the feature. However, there are some conventions and devices that can help capture and maintain reader interest.

94

First, feature style is usually an abrupt departure from news style. The summary lead has limited use, except in modified form on some news features. Use of the inverted pyramid form is rare. When both are used, the story usually is heavy on information and light on human interest — a slightly featurized news story, in essence.

Read the lead and first few paragraphs of this news feature:

MOSCOW (AP) — Soviet press and propaganda organs hammer away these days at rising food prices in the West in an attempt to portray a decline in the Western economic system. But they seldom mention what food costs in the Soviet Union.

The reason for the omission is that the Soviet housewife pays considerably more than housewives in Western countries for food.

One example from the Soviet press was contained in a recent Pravda article. The Communist party organ said: "The food crisis, like all the other present ills of the Western economy, shows the depth and insolubility of the contradictions tearing asunder the capitalist world."

It claimed that big monopolies are making huge profits as food prices rise, and the working people in the West pay dearly for it.

But when one compares the lot of Soviet and Western consumers, the Soviet Union looks a lot worse in the area of food costs.

A list of 11 typical marketbasket items that cost $12.50 in a New York supermarket, according to an Associated Press check, would cost $17.32 in Moscow. But there is much more to it than that.

Emphasis in the first two paragraphs is that Soviet media stress rising prices in the West but omit that housewives in the Soviet Union pay more for food.

The story uses a _____ lead. The story contains more

_____ than human interest.

15–15 summary
information

15–16   Some features use a modified summary lead, but then delay an important part of the information until the end, as a punch line.

Read this news feature:

BOSTON (AP) — The state Weather Amendment Board is going out of business in July. It seems the board, which is responsible for licensing rainmakers, hasn't issued any licenses for 11 years.

Minutes of its rare meetings can't be found. Nor can anyone locate the "systematic assembly of pertinent scientific data" it was supposed to collect.

Its demise won't take much of a load off the state treasury: The agency has spent only $123.42 in its entire 23-year history.

That the agency has spent only $123.42 could have been included in the

lead, but it is _____ until the end to entice the reader through

the entire story.

15–16 delayed

15–17   This "delay" concept is an important one. Feature leads are used to arouse interest, and the body often incorporates a delayed interest technique with a punch line or "kicker" at the end.

Read this news feature:

PANAMA CITY, Fla. (AP) — Whoever burglarized the American Scrap Metal Co. here wasn't deterred by the junkyard's dog.

Police said the culprit used a cutting torch to gain entry to the safe after climbing the metal fence which surrounds the junkyard.

Officers said the burglar took $284 in cash, a .32 cal. pistol, a 1967 car parked near the office — and the German shepherd attack dog posted outside the door.

The lead includes the information that the burglars weren't deterred by the dog, but the fact that _____ is delayed to the last paragraph.

15–17   the dog was stolen

15–18   The lead includes some idea of the nature of the story and gives the reader just enough information to whet the appetite.

Many short news features (3–5 paragraphs) then delay the outcome until the last paragraph. The stolen-dog story is an example of this.

In longer features the outcome usually is placed fairly close to the lead, anywhere from the second to about the fifth paragraph.

The outcome in the short feature often is placed in the _____ as a kicker. The outcome of the longer story usually is placed near the _____.

15–18   last paragraph
    lead

15–19   Which of the following leads do you think would best arouse reader interest? _____

A. Dawn, the government's newest whooping crane, pecked a tiny hole in its shell shortly before sunrise Wednesday — thereby getting its name.

It worked 24 hours enlarging the hole and finally emerged into the world at 7:30 a.m. Thursday.

B. Dawn, the first of the second generation of federal captive-bred whooping cranes, emerged from its shell at 7:30 a.m. Thursday.

With its addition, there are now 28 whooping cranes in captivity and 49 reported in the wild.

C. Being a day-old whooping crane means problems.

Not only does no one know your sex, but there is the publicity and having to remember you're not a turkey.

15–19   Lead C was the UPI lead. (Dawn will be raised with turkey chicks.) Lead A is a fairly descriptive lead, but it doesn't have the "teaser" elements in the second paragraph, as does C. Lead B is almost a straight news approach; it doesn't explain the name.

15–20   In the delayed-interest news feature, a summary or modified summary lead often is followed by chronological development and a kicker at the end.

Read this news feature:

SALT LAKE CITY (UPI) — A red-faced 32-year-old Salt Lake man who spent more than six hours hanging upside down by his ankles said he crawled into the ventilation system of his old high school and got stuck.

Fire department paramedics were called to West High School just as classes were letting out after a student finally found the source of mysterious tapping noises which had filtered through the school all day.

The medics ripped out part of the vent and saw a pair of feet. "I thought he was dead," said paramedic Michael Jessop.

A couple of tugs on the feet produced a tired, sore and embarrassed Marty Martindale, who said he had gone into the vent on a dare from "an old high school buddy."

The story has a modified summary lead, a kicker at the end (a dare from an old high school buddy) and the body developed in _____ order.

15–20   chronological

15–21   The concept that there are no rules for feature writing certainly applies to the lead. We've looked at several summary or modified summary leads that served as teasers to draw the reader through the story.

Others that are used regularly are the narrative, direct address, direct quote or partial quote, question and contrast. There are so many novelty or freak leads that they defy classification.

15–22   The narrative lead is a word picture that sets the stage for the story. It is generally pure description and sometimes has slightly longer sentences and paragraphs so a leisurely pace is achieved:

> NEWINGTON, Conn. (AP) — High atop a hill overlooking the Berlin Turnpike is a spot where many have been laid to rest in the past 20 years. There are plastic flowers on the graves, and the epitaphs bespeak love and devotion of the highest degree.
> But no one is buried there.
> It is the cemetery of the Connecticut Humane Society, and here lie the geese, horses, cats and dogs that became as close as people to the families who owned them.

The narrative beginning shouldn't stretch out so that it unnecessarily delays bringing in the story angle.

The _____ lead sets the stage for the story with a word picture.

15–22   narrative

15–23   The direct address lead either states the *you* or implies it:

> Don't worry about long lines if you haven't bought new license tags. This year you can do it by mail.

A direct address lead should only be used with stories that have universal appeal. Read this lead:

> Maybe you've wondered if the new techniques of "natural birth" are for you, but a nationally known obstetrician contends there's no such thing as "unnatural birth."

Would this lead attract the general newspaper audience? _____ (yes/no).

15–23   No. Certainly it's of little concern to most male readers.

15–24   Quotes work well for feature leads if they are strong enough to command reader interest and if they briefly give an idea of the story content. These are all AP leads:

A.   CHICAGO (AP) — The wanderlust odyssey of Squeak, a Siamese cat, finally ended when Mary Wilkinson was told: "Your cat has crossed the Atlantic five times."

B.   DES MOINES (AP) — "The day I found it, I didn't turn my back on anybody," says Bruce Henderson, still stunned by the $25,000 he found.

C. MONKEY'S EYEBROW, Ky. (AP) — "I told Sissy to come on," said 3-year-old Casey Thomas, who dragged his 18-month-old sister more than 40 feet through a burning mobile home.

Notice that all these leads include summary information tied in with direct quotes.

Also, notice that persons are seldom identified in feature leads. This technique helps the reader understand that it isn't hard news. The only identifications are in story _____.

15–24   C

15–25   The question lead is similar to the direct address lead in that the subject should have broad reader appeal. It is particularly appropriate when the story deals with a problem or a question:

How can an increase in city utility rates be avoided and at the same time residents receive services they now have?
That's the question the Citizen's Advisory Board has been wrestling with for six months . . . .

A question lead can be appropriate when the story concerns a question or a _____.

Be sure you don't write a question no one is likely to ask:

Ever wondered about the Model-T renovation business in Southeastern Oklahoma?

15–25   problem

15–26   Using the direct address or question approach is tempting when nothing else immediately comes to mind. Give the lead some thought and time — in choosing any lead be sure it is the most effective and most appropriate one for the story.

Using the question or the direct address approach may be the easiest way to handle the lead, but neither may be the most _____ or the most _____ for a particular story.

15–26   effective   appropriate

15–27   The contrast lead is most often used in comparing the past with the present:

OMAHA — Mary Clark was apprehensive when she enrolled at the College of St. Mary three years ago. She was 39 and had nine children.
She wondered if she could compete and handle all the demands, and if her family would accept the new situation.
Now Mrs. Clark is president of the student body, attending full time and carrying a B-plus average in art and elementary education. She has been active in numerous campus groups and has been president of several organizations.

The time span can be short, from last week to this week. But regardless of the length of time, the contrast lead compares _____ with present.

15–27   past

15–28   The contrast lead has been used so extensively in magazine features and publicity releases that many writers avoid it or seek to modify it. This lead provides contrast and plays down the time element:

HOMESTEAD, Fla. (AP) — Barbara Fuller was picking tomatoes in a muddy field just after she bore her fifth child last year, wishing there was some way an untrained field hand could find a clean, dependable job.

A few months later, she and 19 other migrant women stepped onto a stage and received certificates as trained nurse's aides, guarantees they would not have to return to the backbreaking labor most of them had known since childhood.

This lead is a _____ of the contrast lead.

15–28   modification

15–29   Important devices used in the body of the feature story are transitions, anecdotes, figures of speech, show 'n tell and little person–big picture.

15–30   Feature writers have to assume their stories will be run fully, not trimmed here and there; therefore, they can use transitions to link paragraphs, producing a smooth story flow.

The technique is to tie the first sentence of the paragraph with the last sentence of the preceding paragraph.

The transition is placed in the _____ sentence of the paragraph.

15–30   first

15–31   Here are examples:

A.   "I just want to keep my old hoe-down music alive," he said.
"Bluegrass music is just country music spiced up a bit like cake on Sunday morning."
It was the spice that kept the crowd jumping at the three-day weekend Bluegrass special . . . .

B.   The flood of water and coal mine refuse that cascaded down the hollow after a huge slag pile dam gave way killed 118 persons and left 4,000 homeless.
It also washed away the Appalachian valley's sense of community, leaving the survivors bitter, suspicious and lonely, the researchers said . . . .

The transition in story A is *spice;* the transition in story B is

_____.

15–31   It also washed (away)

15–32   It is especially important to use transitions between major parts of the story. If you divide the story into several topics, a

_____ definitely is needed to take the reader from one topic to the next.

15–32   transition

15–33   Anecdotes are brief descriptions of interesting incidents or events. The anecdote is a key device to keep the feature interesting and to keep it moving when it could bog down in paraphrases and quotes.

People are the prime subjects for features. Even with stories about things, much of the information has to come from interviews with persons connected with them.

The interesting stories people have to tell are used as

_____ to keep the story moving.

15–33 anecdotes

15–34 The anecdote also is useful to prevent the writer from drawing conclusions for the reader.

For example, a reporter has ridden on patrol with two police officers, and from the interview information decides the story angle is the dedication of the policeman in spite of low pay, bad hours, danger and sometimes low prestige.

Spelling out this dedication in the copy would be amateurish. It would be better to use anecdotes and let readers draw their own conclusions.

Used properly, anecdotes reveal what makes a person tick, and the writer avoids drawing _____.

15–34 conclusions

15–35 Feature writing style is much more conversational than the style used for straight news. It can be very casual, depending on the content. A humorous feature is handled in light, casual fashion, whereas a feature dealing with a tragedy will be straightforward.

Read this story and underline the casual expressions:

LOS ANGELES (UPI) — One brown prefabricated house remained at large Saturday after eight police detectives scoured south central Los Angeles with nary a trace of the structure.

"I told my detectives, 'Look, if we can't find a house, we can't find anything,'" said Police Sgt. A. E. Corgan.

"One thing is for sure. It has been broken down into a package and it hasn't been reassembled yet," Corgan said.

Police believed the housenapping occurred late Wednesday from its lot.

Friday, police issued an all points bulletin for "one brown house with dura-plywood exterior."

15–35 remained at large
nary a trace
housenapping

15–36 Figures of speech and analogies can make concepts more understandable. Use fresh ones and avoid clichés.

Most figurative language used by journalists is direct comparison:

The mayor is like a veteran prizefighter.

It's not the first time Jones has donned his armor and entered the arena.

Underline the figures of speech in this excerpt:

GAINESVILLE — The heat shimmers up from the dirt and asphalt that used to be grass at Florida Field.

Workers, wearing straw stetsons, eat lunch under the stands and stare out at the state's yellow road graders and trucks.

The black base for Florida's new artificial turf is near completion. Plans are to put down the fuzzy grass July 6. It'll be a wall-to-wall sea of green. If you'd put the stuff in your house, it would cost about $25 a yard or so — that is, if you were buying enough to cover a football field.

It's great stuff, they say. Dogs can't dig it up. It doesn't need water except before games when it's too hot to play on. You don't cut it — just sort of zip it on like it was a green cocktail dress. And like a Paris original, it's got class — $200,000 worth.

With the planting of this plastic pasture comes a new era, an era almost glittering under a set of $80,000 lights (they don't quite work yet), of blinking scoreboards, flags and fresh paint — just like a shiny new Christmas toy.

They call the turf Doug's Rug, after football coach Doug Dickey, now in his sophomore year at Florida. A harsh word hits him like cigarette ashes on it . . . .

15–36 *Paragraph 3:* sea of green. *Paragraph 4:* it was a green cocktail dress; like a Paris original. *Paragraph 5:* plastic pasture; just like a shiny new Christmas toy. *Paragraph 6:* hits him like cigarette ashes on it

15–37 To review, what kind of lead is used in the story in frame 15–36? _____

15–37 narrative/descriptive

15–38 The show 'n tell device simply describes what a person is doing while he is speaking. The purpose is to break up a long direct quote and to inject action in a long series of direct quotations.

"Now the work really begins," Smith said, pointing to a foot-tall stack of computer printouts on the window ledge. "Those represent about 500 hours of interviewing time and we just hope it won't take that many more hours to analyze the data."

The purpose of this device is to give action to a series of quotes and to _____ a long direct quote.

15–38 break up

15–39 A useful feature lead technique is the little person–big picture. One person or a small group of persons are used in the lead paragraphs to represent a large population that will be described in the body of the story — like a case study representative of many cases.

The little person–big picture technique uses a person or small group to be _____ of a larger group.

15–39 representative

15–40 The little person–big picture technique is most applicable when the story is heavy on data and statistics. It leads off as a "people" story, not a statistical story.

Also, it can provide a fresh approach to a story about a group or organization where there really isn't a fresh angle. For example, a story about a drug halfway house can lead with a case study of a person to humanize and lend interest.

When the story is heavy with _____, the little person–big picture is a good approach.

15–40 data/statistics

15–41 The little person–big picture technique applies well to stories dealing with social problems.

In the example that follows, the little person is brought into the lead; then, a transition in the fourth paragraph ties her in with the big picture — 70,000 senior citizens:

MIAMI BEACH (UPI) — Mayee Phillips, 71, had been standing in the free-lunch line for two hours. She was sweating and her feet were aching. The mid-day sun and gnawing emptiness in her stomach had quickened her breathing.

But the worst pain was yet to come.

When the doors to the Metropolitan Senior Center finally opened, the crowd of 200 surged forward, pushing, shoving and jostling for position.

She was knocked to the pavement and kicked. By the time she recovered the 150 meal tickets were long gone, and she went home to join 70,000 other Miami-area senior citizens who go to bed hungry every night.

"It's like this most days," said Helen Breen, president of the Metropolitan Senior Center — one of eight in Dade County that provide one free hot meal a day for 3,000 senior citizens.

"They're like children fighting among themselves at the door. But for many of them it's their only meal of the day."

A strong transition is required with this technique. It ties in the little

person with the _____.

15–41	big picture	**15–42** Features are a personal kind of journalism, compared with the hard news story. Literary structures and devices are used frequently and the writer has considerable freedom in deciding how to handle the story.

15–42   Features are a personal kind of journalism, compared with the hard news story. Literary structures and devices are used frequently and the writer has considerable freedom in deciding how to handle the story.

But, regardless of style, the feature writer is still reporting facts, not writing an opinion piece.

The feature isn't creative writing with overtones of journalism; it is

reporting _____ in a style that makes use of literary devices.

15–42   facts

15–43   The freedom involved in feature writing is coupled with an equal amount of responsibility. Be sure your approach and techniques are appropriate. Tone has to be appropriate — one story may be somber, another may be funny. The tone has to correspond to the facts, and it has to be consistent.

A key word in the writer's decision making is _____.

15–43   appropriateness

15–44   The feature may sometimes have a theme — a single element used throughout the story to unify it.

Find the theme in the following: _____

HONOLULU (AP) — For Larry Windley, the sea was both friend and foe. And he loved it.

"When I go, if I go," he once told a sailing friend, "I hope to hell it's in the ocean."

Windley, 36, left his native North Carolina in 1956 and came here to seek a living as an underwater photographer and professional diver.

He founded a diving firm two years later on the island of Maui and was credited with starting Hawaii's black coral industry.

But the warm Pacific he loved so much demanded a heavy toll.

Nearly 10 years ago, Windley emerged from a deep dive with a near-fatal seizure of bends. It left him paralyzed from the neck down.

Though he never got back the use of his legs, Windley eventually could get around on crutches.

Unable to return to the sea for a living, Windley became active in Maui civic affairs. He backed plans to restore Lahaina to its appearance of the

1800s when the missionaries arrived and he helped organize the annual Lahaina Whaling Spree.

He didn't own a boat anymore, but he had dozens of seagoing buddies and the ocean remained a big part of his life.

One of them, St. George Bryan, a Maui resident, invited Windley out last Thursday for a brief cruise around Molokini Island in his small catamaran.

Neither has been seen since.

Despite an air and sea search, the Coast Guard found no trace of the craft. The search has been called off.

15–44   the sea (friend and foe)

15–45   The Windley story uses the _____ interest technique of placing the outcome at the end.

15–45   delayed

15–46   The body of the story is developed in a natural time sequence, or _____ order.

15–46   chronological

15–47   The Windley story illustrates the reporter's perceptiveness and willingness to dig for information.

The story could have been handled routinely in hard news style from Coast Guard sources. Instead it is developed into a good feature.

1.   Choose the most interesting, appropriate lead:

        A. LONDON — Horse talk has long interested Henry Blake. So he has translated their signs and sounds into English in dictionary form.

        B. LONDON — "Come on," said the horse, "where's my bloody breakfast?"

           Henry Blake didn't blink an eye. Horses speak to him so clearly that he has compiled what he calls the world's first dictionary of equine language.

        C. LONDON — Ever wonder what horses are saying?

           Henry Blake says he understands horse talk. In fact, he's compiled a dictionary of horse language translated into English.

2.   Choose the best lead:

        A. SPIVEY'S CORNER, N.C. — Spivey's Corner, not even a speck on North Carolina's map, will be one of the noisiest places on earth June 21 when the seventh annual National Hollerin' Contest begins.

        B. SPIVEY'S CORNER, N.C. — Do you sometimes get the urge to let off steam?

           Then you should get in on the action here June 21 when the seventh annual National Hollerin' Contest begins.

        C. SPIVEY'S CORNER, N.C. — Noise will be the featured attraction here June 21 when the seventh annual National Hollerin' Contest begins.

3.   Stories about well-known places and things usually require some kind of angle to capture reader interest. _____ (true/false)

4.   Inverted pyramid form is rarely used in the feature. _____ (true/false)

5.   A "kicker" is part of a feature lead. _____ (true/false)

6.   Where is the outcome of the short news feature commonly placed? _____

7.   Delayed interest and _____ order are common structural forms for the body of the story.

8. Persons seldom are identified in feature leads. _____ (true/false)

9. The direct address lead and _____ lead are appropriate for a subject with broad reader appeal.

10. The _____ lead compares past with present.

11. _____ connect paragraphs and produce a smooth story flow.

12. Anecdotes help keep the story interesting and keep it _____.

13. The show 'n tell device breaks up a long direct quote and injects _____ in a series of quotes.

14. The little person–big picture device is useful when there isn't a fresh story angle and when the _____.

15. The little person–big picture story requires a _____ between the lead and the body.

answers

1. B
2. A
3. false
4. true
5. false
6. at the end
7. chronological
8. true
9. question
10. contrast
11. transitions
12. moving
13. action
14. story has considerable data, statistics
15. transition